The MULTIPLE INTELLIGENCES
of Reading and Writing

Making the Words Come Alive

Thomas Armstrong

T 74090

Association for Supervision and Curriculum Development
Alexandria, Virginia USA

Association for Supervision and Curriculum Development
1703 N. Beauregard St. • Alexandria, VA 22311-1714 USA
Telephone: 800-933-2723 or 703-578-9600 • Fax: 703-575-5400
Web site: http://www.ascd.org • E-mail: member@ascd.org

Gene R. Carter, *Executive Director;* Nancy Modrak, *Director of Publishing;* Julie Houtz, *Director of Book Editing & Production;* Deborah Siegel, *Project Manager;* Reece Quiñones, *Senior Graphic Designer;* Keith Demmons, *Typesetter;* Dina Seamon, *Production Specialist.*

All Web links in this book are correct as of the publication date below but may have become inactive or otherwise modified since that time. If you notice a deactivated or changed link, please e-mail books@ascd.org with the words "Link Update" in the subject line. In your message, please specify the Web link, the book title, and the page number on which the link appears.

Printed in the United States of America.

April 2003 member book (pc). ASCD Premium, Comprehensive, and Regular members periodically receive ASCD books as part of their membership benefits. No. FY03-06.

ISBN: 0-87120-718-4   ASCD product no.: 102280   ASCD member price: $ 18.95   nonmember price: $ 22.95

Library of Congress Cataloging-in-Publication Data

Armstrong, Thomas.
  The multiple intelligences of reading and writing : making the words
come alive / Thomas Armstrong.
      p. cm.
Includes bibliographical references (p.   ) and index.
  ISBN 0-87120-718-4 (alk. paper)
  1. Language arts. 2. Multiple intelligences. 3. Literacy. I. Title.

LB1576.A713 2002
372.6--dc21
                                                    2002154699

08 07 06 05 04 03   10 9 8 7 6 5 4 3 2 1

To my sister Bonnie, who opened up worlds of authors for me when I was young.

The MULTIPLE INTELLIGENCES of Reading and Writing

Making the Words Come Alive

Introduction

This book has its origins in two separate but related issues in my life, one a joyful personal experience and the other a professional conundrum. First, let me speak of the joyful experience. About five years ago, I happened to be watching a videotape of the Al Pacino film *Looking for Richard*. In this picture, which is part documentary and part Shakespearean performance, Pacino takes the viewer through the various stages of putting on the play *Richard III*. We see the actors meeting to discuss roles, we hear interviews with people on the street concerning their feelings about Shakespeare, we see Pacino himself commenting on the play and its history, and we get, of course, several scenes from the play itself. Seeing this picture was a kind of miraculous turning point for me in my intellectual life. Before this, I had not been much of a reader since college 25 years earlier.

Just to give you a sense of where I was at with literacy, when I was a teacher in the public school system I remember taking some courses for the purpose of obtaining a salary increment, but I was so lazy or so "a-literate" (able to read but choosing not to) that I read the *Cliffs Notes* instead of the actual texts. After seeing *Looking for Richard*, however, I started to read Shakespeare's plays. I read the mass-market paperback versions put out by the Folger Shakespeare Library in Washington, D.C. I liked them because they put the explanations of difficult words and phrases on the facing page instead of in footnotes at the bottom of the page (this arrangement prevented me from getting dizzy or headachy through moving my head up and down all the time). I devoured most of the plays in a matter of months. I loved them!

After Shakespeare's plays, I went on to other books and authors. I became interested in the whole Western cultural tradition. I purchased taped courses from The Teaching Company (www.teach12.com), an organization that tapes lectures from some of the best college professors in the country on a variety of topics in the humanities and the sciences. I especially loved the taped lectures on American and British literature by Professor Arnold Weinstein of Brown University. I began (finally) to do the reading for my courses. I fell in love with Plato's *The Republic* and Dante's *The Divine Comedy*, with Rabelais, with the Argentinean writer Jorge Luis Borges (the Rod Serling of the international literary world), with Hemingway, Faulkner, Marcus Aurelius, Thomas More, Homer, Thoreau, Dickens, Woolf, Joyce, Austen, Ellison, Morrison; books became like salted peanuts to me. I just couldn't stop! The time that I had been spending before bedtime flipping through the several hundred channels of my cable system, I now spent reading. And it's amazing how much reading a person can do in a few years if he reads for just an hour or two a day. At any rate, what I'm trying to say is that after 25 years as an educator, I finally started to become truly literate myself. This naturally filled me with a desire to share my joy in some way with the world. So, the idea of writing a book that would help children and adults learn how to read and write, so that they too could experience the wonder and excitement of the written word, seemed very appropriate to me as a next step in my own development.

Now, on to the conundrum. Back in the late 1980s, when the theory of multiple intelligences (MI theory) was still in its infancy and I was beginning to do workshops for educators on this emerging topic, I was often asked a question that made me uncomfortable. Though it was asked in different ways, the basic question almost always took something close to the following form: "Both you and Howard Gardner say that there are many different ways to learn and teach. But right now you are lecturing to us about multiple intelligences in only one intelligence: linguistic intelligence. Doesn't that tell us that this particular intelligence is the most important one?" There would usually be a momentary silence, following which I would hem and haw and tell them that, if I wanted to, I could sing to them about multiple intelligences, dance the multiple intelligences, draw the multiple intelligences, and so forth. But the fact is, I didn't. Over time, in part as a response to this question, I learned to incorporate all the intelligences into my workshops so that participants *would* be singing, chanting, dancing, drawing, visualizing, and in other ways using all eight of Gardner's intelligences. The fact that I did this, coupled with the increasing acceptance of MI theory as a mainstream concept in education, eventually caused this question to go away. Nowadays, I almost never get asked a question like this at my workshops. Perhaps I should shout "Hurrah! I made the bad question go away!" and go on to other matters. The truth is, however, that I am still troubled by the question, and even quietly disappointed that nobody asks it very much anymore. Because I think the question is still a valid one and quite fundamental to the ongoing discourse on multiple intelligences.

Consider the following. Gardner initially introduced the theory of multiple intelligences to the world through a book: *Frames of Mind*. This book received many awards, tremendous media publicity (incredible for a book on education), and was ultimately named by *Education Week* as one of the 100 most influential education books of the 20th century. One might argue persuasively that the entire theory of multiple intelligences, and the great changes that it has evoked in thousands of schools worldwide, originally emerged from this single *linguistic* product. Add to this comments by Gardner to interviewers that his own teaching style at the Harvard School of Education relies heavily on lectures and reading. Further consider that although there are multimedia products, videos, and other nonlinguistic resources available for communicating about the concepts of multiple intelligences, the vast bulk of materials on MI theory are in the form of books, articles, audiotapes, and other *linguistic* sources. Finally, it should be noted that although I do involve my workshop participants actively in all eight of the intelligences, the largest part of my workshops, by far, are taken up by my own lectures, group discussions, questions and answers, and handouts—all of them, *linguistic* teaching strategies. It might also be added, almost parenthetically, that what you are holding in your hands right now also is a linguistic product: a *book* that is attempting to come to grips with all of this.

What if Gardner had originally decided to present his ideas about multiple intelligences in the form of a song? Would anybody have listened? What if he had choreographed the concept and presented it as a dance at a large theater hall? Would anybody have showed up? What I am trying to point out here is that the question I was so bothered about in my early workshops is still alive and deserves to be brought to the surface and openly debated in the fullest possible way. There seems to be a basic contradiction when it comes to the actual practice of the theory of multiple intelligences. On the one hand, we say that students should be able to learn and be taught in many different intelligences. On the other hand, when we look at what our culture actually *does*, what it values most, what it spends most of its time focusing on, we find *linguistic* intelligence far ahead of the pack. (One might successfully argue a case for the primacy of logical-mathematical intelligence, as well, in our culture. However, consider what would have happened if Gardner had originally introduced MI theory as a series of equations or algorithms. Would anybody have cared? Would anybody have been able to figure them out?)

It's certainly possible to argue, as I and many others have, that while our culture may value linguistic intelligence above the other seven, it certainly *shouldn't* continue to do so. The theory of multiple intelligences, in this view, serves as a critique of the values of our schools and our culture, suggesting that we need to pay much more attention to the neglected intelligences, especially those such as spatial, bodily-kinesthetic, musical, and naturalist, that may be particular strengths of individuals who have had special difficulties in successfully making their way through our heavily linguistic schools. Taken in this manner, MI theory serves as an important impetus toward fundamental reforms of our educational system, leading to a re-evaluation of those subjects typically taught in school, with increased emphasis placed on the arts, nature, physical culture, and other topics traditionally limited to the periphery of the curriculum.

I continue to argue for such substantial reforms. However, there is also a part of me that understands and accepts the situation, perhaps more fully than before, that linguistic intelligence happens to be what is most valued right now. And not *just* right now. I would argue that since the beginning of recorded time, linguistic intelligence has held sway in an imposing manner over the other seven intelligences. In fact, by definition, recorded time began when people first recorded information through the written word. We have cave drawings going back tens of thousands of years. We have simple tools going back much farther than that. However, archeologists are unable to reconstruct a clear sense of what individuals were thinking about in those ancient times just by looking at these artifacts, despite a valiant attempt to do so through the emerging field of cognitive archeology. And yet, we *can* get inside the thoughts of a Sumerian scribe living almost 5,000 years ago when he wrote these words in ancient cuneiform to his menial assistant: "You dolt, numbskull, school pest, you Sumerian ignoramus, your hand is terrible; it cannot even hold the stylus properly; it is unfit for writing and cannot even take dictation. Yet you say you are a scribe like me" (quoted in McGuinness, 1985, p. 234). Some things never change!

From ancient civilizations to the present time, the balance of power has resided in people who were literate. The scribes of early history were closely allied to the rulers and were part of the power elite. Writing about ancient Mayan civilization, for example, Kevin J. Johnston of Ohio State University notes: "Texts were a medium through which kings asserted and displayed power" (Johnston, 2001). For further ancient examples, one has only to think of the Code of Hammurabi, the Ten Commandments, and the inscriptions of the Persian king Darius cut high up into an inaccessible portion of a cliff in western Iran. The ancient writing surface, papyrus, gets its name from an Egyptian word *pa-en-per-aa* meaning "that which belonged to the king" (Robinson, 1995, p. 107). The overwhelming portion of writing from both the ancient and modern worlds was written by those who had shares in the riches and powers of the elite. We will never know what sorts of thoughts, hopes, wishes, needs, or frustrations ran through the minds of millions of slaves, poor farmers, artisans, soldiers, wives, and other dispossessed peoples during the vast majority of recorded history, because these individuals were never given the opportunity to develop literacy.

In the present day, literacy continues to serve as a requirement for membership in the upper classes in most parts of the world. Educators such as Paulo Freire have argued persuasively that literacy represents a key tool for social change, and for the empowerment of oppressed peoples (Freire, 2000). In American culture, those individuals who are at the top of the social structure are those who are most fully literate, and conversely, those who lack literacy skills occupy the lowest rungs of the social ladder. You can go into a cocktail party and make people laugh empathetically with a comment like: "Gee, I've never been able to balance my checkbook" or "I've never been able to dance (or draw) well." But try saying "Gee, I've never learned how to read or write" and imagine what kind of response you're likely to get. Stunned silence, most likely. Not to be able to read in our culture is a source of shame and humiliation for many. One can say this is society's fault, and that we put too much emphasis on words in our culture, but those are the facts and we have to live and deal with the situation and what it means for the students who are in our charge. Whether we like it or not, one of the best things that we as educators can do to help our students achieve success in this culture is to assist them in becoming as fully literate as possible.

Now, however, we encounter another sort of difficulty. Many children and adults in America struggle with reading and writing, both in school and as a part of normal living outside of school. According to a study done by the Yale School of Medicine, some 20 percent of American school children—or 10 million kids—have some kind of "reading disorder" (Shaywitz, Escobar, Shaywitz, Fletcher, & Makuch, 1992). The assessment of 4th grade reading conducted as part of the National Assessment of Educational Progress (NAEP) in 2000 shows declines from previous years among the poorest readers, while all other groups at higher levels of reading proficiency show stable patterns of achievement or even increases over time (Donahue, Finnegan, Lutkus, Allen, & Campell, 2001). A recent National Institute for Literacy report suggests that 40 to 44 million Americans are "functionally illiterate." Clearly, the problem of literacy is a national dilemma.

Educators, researchers, scientists, and others have written extensively on why so many people in the United States struggle with literacy, despite the fact that we have one of the most highly developed educational systems in the world. Some suggest that social inequities are the cause. Others point to neurological abnormalities of genetic origin. Some indicate that not enough phonics is the culprit. Others put forth still newer theories to prove their case. What we really need, however, are not reasons or excuses for why so many children and adults are not literate, but rather positive solutions for helping empower everyone with the skills of literacy. It is here where I believe the theory of multiple intelligences can, curiously, make one of its most valuable contributions to education. In this book, I advocate an approach to literacy based on the belief that there is no one best way to teach reading and writing skills, in part because each person is so differently organized neurologically, and that the best attitude to adopt in any literacy program is a multiple-solution focus. In this book I show that reading and writing are not simply linguistic acts; they involve all of the intelligences, and many more areas of the brain are involved in literacy acquisition than has previously been assumed by educators working in the field. We have limited ourselves too much in the past—even in the field of MI theory—by considering too narrow a range of interventions, and ignoring many other strategies that are available for helping children and adults acquire literacy skills.

Reading and writing are unique evolutionary features of the human species that represent the tail end of a long and carefully articulated process of development over time. I show in this book how literacy emerged out of our oral language capacities, our logical capabilities, our physical movements, our image making abilities, our musical proclivities, our emotional life, our attempts to decipher and control nature, and our impulse to connect meaningfully with others. Moreover, I point out how reading and writing, while definitely distinctive activities in their own right, still retain close connections to these broader aspects of human potential. Literacy is far too recent a development in human life for it to be otherwise. I suggest that a revolution of sorts is required in the way that we think about reading and writing, so that more of the brain's power may be brought to bear upon the acquisition of these valued skills.

The first chapter summarizes the basics of multiple intelligences theory, and provides an overview of the connections that reading and writing have with different areas of the brain, including not simply those areas typically tied to language functions (e.g., Broca's area, Wernicke's area), but also with areas associated with emotion, music, imagery, and motor activity. Each subsequent chapter examines the relationship of reading and writing to a different intelligence within MI theory. Following Howard Gardner's approach in *Frames of Mind*, each of these chapters begins with a section that connects a particular intelligence to literacy through research in the brain sciences, developmental psychology, evolutionary studies, biographies of creative individuals, cognitive psychology, and other fields. The larger part of each chapter, however, is devoted to practical strategies that exploit the resources of that particular intelligence for teaching reading and writing skills to children or adults. There is no attempt to pit one approach over another—to claim, for example, that a phonics approach is better than a whole-word method or a whole-language approach. In fact, phonetic strategies will be covered in *each* chapter, because each of the eight intelligences provides different ways of helping learners acquire the all-important knowledge of sound-symbol relationships. The structure of the applied section of each chapter moves from micro to macro in its coverage of practical strategies. Beginning with *letters and sounds,* we then move on to *whole words,* then *whole sentences,* then to *bodies of text,* then to selecting appropriate *books and other literacy materials* that integrate linguistic text with the intelligence of that chapter, and finally conclude with the broader treatment of general *literacy styles* that might be associated with each of the eight intelligences. Many of the activities and ideas associated with a wide range of approaches to teaching reading and writing, and to specific literacy programs are also cited in each chapter.

The emphasis here is to be inclusive and to not waste time on which system or method or program is best, but rather to see the best aspects of each way of teaching reading and writing—and to understand why certain methods work best with certain students and not with others. The theory of multiple intelligences and its neurological underpinnings, I believe, reveal the power of certain literacy strategies to work miracles with those individuals who have previously been thought to have intractable difficulties when it came to learning to read or write (and where various labels such as "dyslexic," "learning disabled," and "reading disordered" have been used to explain away their supposed incapacity to learn).

It is my hope that this book will be a helpful supplementary resource for educators seeking to expand their repertoire of strategies for engaging students in reading and writing, whether they be regular classroom teachers, learning disability specialists, speech and language pathologists, reading teachers, Title I personnel, bilingual or ESOL educators, private tutors, literacy volunteers, parents, or anyone else interested in helping others experience the satisfactions of literacy. My special wish is that this book will serve as a doorway for educators who are seeking to reach students who have had difficulty with traditional methods of learning to read and write. If this book helps just a few students learn to read and write who otherwise might have been frustrated in their attempts, or makes the journey toward literacy come alive for students who might otherwise have considered it drudgery, I will have accomplished my goal, which is to share my own deep love of literacy with others.

1

Literacy, Multiple Intelligences, and the Brain

Most of us are familiar with the story of the Blind Men and the Elephant, a tale that comes to us from ancient India. In this story, a king presented an elephant to a number of blind men in his community and asked each to say what he thought it was. The first man touched the side of the beast and answered, "A wall." The second walked up and felt a leg, and replied, "No, this is a pillar." A third man encountered the tail and cried out, "This is certainly not a wall nor a pillar! It's a rope!" A fourth man latched on to an ear and exclaimed: "You're all wrong! It's a piece of cloth!" And the men began arguing and fighting among themselves about who was really right.

Recently, I discovered another related story that isn't nearly as well known. It's entitled "The Blind Educators and the Literacy Lion." In this story (which has rather fuzzier origins), a king asks several blind educators in his village to examine a new beast that has come into his possession and to tell him all about it. The first educator goes up to touch the Literacy Lion, and then runs back to the king shouting: "This beast is made up of whole words! Yes, all sorts of words, like *the* and *captain* and *sure* and *poultry* and *wizard* and tens of thousands more!" Then the king signaled for the second educator to go up to the Literacy Lion, which she did, and after some time she returned to the king saying: "This animal isn't made of whole words! It's made up of sounds! All kinds of sounds! Sounds like 'thhhh' and 'buh' and 'ahhhhh' and 'ayyyyy' and 'juh' and many more. In fact, I counted all the sounds, and there are exactly 44!" A third educator was sent to examine the beast, and he returned and exclaimed: "This creature isn't made up of sounds or whole words. It's constructed out of stories, and fables, and songs, and chants, and poems, and storybooks, and Big Books, and board books, and novels, and plays, and whole libraries full of living, exciting tales, and lots more besides!" Finally, a fourth educator was sent, and she came back saying: "They're all wrong! This beast is made up of whole cultures, and people crying out for freedom and power, and it's about understanding who we are and what we're capable of, and how each of us can speak, and read, and write with our own voices, and in this way contribute to the good of all." And with this final assessment, the educators proceeded to dispute heatedly among themselves.

By now, you will have probably recognized that this story is a thinly disguised attempt to describe the history of literacy acquisition and the teaching of reading and writing over the past several decades in the United States and elsewhere. Beginning in 1955, with the publication of Rudolf Flesch's best-selling book *Why Johnny Can't Read* (Flesch, 1986), a series of disputes erupted in educational circles regarding the best way to teach literacy. This controversy is sometimes referred to as "The Reading Wars." In this dispute, each combatant claims that his or her particular approach, whether it be phonics, basal readers, whole language, critical literacy, or any of a number of other methods, represents the single best way to teach reading, writing, or both to our students. A lot of ink has been spilled in the course of this battle, and despite rounds and rounds of negotiations, the war continues to this day.

I think it's time to put an end to these reading wars. The Literacy Lion is a powerful, complex, and mysterious beast. Each description that we receive of it—from educators, psychologists, brain researchers, and other professionals—can only enrich our knowledge of what this powerful being is really made of, and why we want so much for our students to have contact with it. In this book, I would like to attempt an integration of the diverse range of perspectives on reading and writing—a sort of peace conference on literacy—so that we might forge ahead as educators united, rather than divided, on this important educational issue. In synthesizing many of the ideas, programs, methods, brain research studies, and other contributions to literacy acquisition, I use Howard Gardner's theory of multiple intelligences (MI theory) as an organizing framework. I want to make it clear from the outset that I do not propose that multiple intelligences now be considered *the* best approach to literacy acquisition. I do not wish to become a new combatant in the reading wars. Rather, I want to use MI theory as a *tool* to help make sense of the many different approaches to reading and writing that are out there, showing how these different methods complement rather than contradict each other. I wish to employ MI theory, then, as a metacognitive strategy for organizing and making sense of the research findings, programs, and strategies that are already out there and being used in the teaching of reading and writing. As we will see, there is a place for each of the many perspectives that have been offered over the past half-century regarding the best way to help students—from early childhood to late adulthood—acquire the skills of literacy.

The Theory of Multiple Intelligences: A Brief Primer

Because I am using multiple intelligences as the unifying element in this peace conference on literacy, I would like to provide a short introduction for the reader who may be unacquainted with the theory. Those who wish to explore the theory in more depth may refer to a number of other resources: Armstrong, 1999a, 2000a, 2000b; Campbell, Campbell, & Dickinson, 1995; Gardner, 1983, 1993, 1999; Hoerr, 2000; Lazear, 1999; Nelson, 1998. The theory of multiple intelligences was developed by Harvard professor Howard Gardner in the early 1980s (Gardner, 1983). Gardner argues that traditional ideas about intelligence employed in educational and psychological circles for almost a hundred years require significant reform. In particular, he suggests that the concept of a "pure" intelligence that can be measured by a single IQ score is seriously flawed. Instead, Gardner points out that intelligence isn't a singular phenomenon, but rather a plurality of capacities. Drawing on his own observations and those of other scholars from several different disciplines, including anthropology, developmental psychology, animal physiology, brain research, cognitive science, and biographies of exceptional individuals, Gardner concluded that there were at least seven different types of intelligences that everyone seems to possess to a greater or lesser degree. As the theory evolved, he added an eighth intelligence to this list (Gardner, 1993). Each intelligence represents a set of capacities that are brought to bear upon two major focuses: the solving of problems, and the fashioning of significant cultural products. These eight intelligences are

1. Linguistic Intelligence. The understanding of the phonology, syntax, and semantics of language, and its pragmatic uses to convince others of a course of action, help one to remember information, explain or communicate knowledge, or reflect upon language itself. Examples include the storyteller, orator, poet, editor, and novelist.

2. Bodily-Kinesthetic Intelligence. The ability to control one's bodily motions and the capacity to handle objects skillfully. Examples of those proficient in this intelligence include the actor, mime, craftsperson, athlete, dancer, and sculptor.

3. Spatial Intelligence. The ability to perceive the visual world accurately, to perform transformations and modifications upon one's initial perceptions, and to be able to re-create aspects of one's visual experience (even in the absence of the relevant physical stimuli). Examples include the architect, mapmaker, surveyor, inventor, and graphic artist.

4. Musical Intelligence. The ability to understand and express components of music, including melodic and rhythmic patterns, through figural or intuitive means (the natural musician) or through formal analytic means (the professional musician). Examples include the composer, pianist, percussionist, music critic, and singer.

5. Logical-Mathematical Intelligence. The understanding and use of logical structures, including patterns and relationships, and statements and propositions, through experimentation, quantification, conceptualization, and classification. Examples include the scientist, mathematician, logician, computer programmer, and statistician.

6. Intrapersonal Intelligence. The ability to access one's own emotional life through awareness of inner moods, intentions, motivations, potentials, temperaments, and desires, and the capacity to symbolize these inner experiences, and to apply these understandings to help one live one's life. Examples include the psychotherapist, entrepreneur, creative artist, and shaman.

7. Interpersonal Intelligence. The ability to notice and make distinctions among other individuals with respect to moods, temperaments, motivations, intentions, and to use this information in pragmatic ways, such as to persuade, influence, manipulate, mediate, or counsel individuals or groups of individuals toward some purpose. Examples include the union organizer, teacher, therapist, administrator, and political leader.

8. Naturalist Intelligence. The capacity to recognize and classify the numerous species of flora and fauna in one's environment (as well as natural phenomena such as mountains and clouds), and the ability to care for, tame, or interact subtly with living creatures, or with whole ecosystems. Examples include the zoologist, biologist, veterinarian, forest ranger, and hunter.

Of primary importance in the construction of MI theory is Gardner's use of a set of eight criteria that need to be met in order for each intelligence to qualify for inclusion on his list (Gardner, 1983). What makes MI theory stand out from a number of other theories of learning and intelligence is the existence of this set of criteria, and the fact that it encompasses a widely diverse range of disciplines—all pointing to the relative autonomy of these eight intelligences. The criteria are

- **Susceptibility to Encoding in a Symbol System.** Gardner suggests that each intelligence has its own unique set of symbol systems. For example, linguistic intelligence includes a wide range of languages such as English, French, Spanish, and Russian, while logical-mathematical intelligence employs number systems and computer languages, and interpersonal intelligence draws upon a diverse group of gestures, facial expressions, and postures to represent moods, intentions, and ideas.

- **Support from Psychometric Findings.** Gardner indicates that if one looks at the subtest scores from standard intelligence tests, or at the quantitative measures for logical, linguistic, artistic, social, emotional, or kinesthetic aptitude tests, evidence suggests a general lack of correlation between scores in different intelligence areas, thus pointing to the relative independence of each intelligence.

- **An Evolutionary History and Evolutionary Plausibility.** A look at the archeological evidence suggests that each of the eight intelligences appears to have been used during prehistoric times by early *homo sapiens*, and most likely were used at even earlier stages of evolution, as evidenced by the presence of these intelligences in other members of the animal kingdom (e.g., musical intelligence in birds, spatial intelligence in bees, interpersonal intelligence in ants).

- **A Distinctive Developmental History and a Definable Set of Expert "End-State" Performances.** Each of the eight intelligences provides numerous examples of high-level achievement in individuals who are at the peak of their discipline (for example, Marie Curie, Georgia O'Keeffe, Virginia Woolf, Martin Luther King, Jr., Auguste Rodin, Jane Goodall, Sigmund Freud, Kiri Te Kanawa), and there appear to be specific stages that individuals go through in traveling along the path from a novice to a master in each domain.

- **The Existence of Savants, Prodigies, and Other Exceptional Individuals.** For each intelligence, there are individuals who have incredible abilities in that particular intelligence and yet appear to be highly underdeveloped in some or most of the other intelligences. For example, the literature includes examples of "savants" who can calculate rapidly in their minds and yet have subnormal IQ scores, those who read difficult text without understanding it (hyperlexia), and five-year-old children who can draw at a gifted adult level, but have significant social impairments such as autism.

- **An Identifiable Core Operation or Set of Operations.** Each intelligence has a definable set of operations that can be enumerated with specificity and taught to another person. For example, bodily-kinesthetic operations may include the ability to imitate the physical movements of others or the capacity to master established fine-motor routines for building a structure. For musical intelligence, operations might involve sensitivity to pitch or the ability to discriminate among different rhythmic patterns.

- **Support from Experimental Psychological Tasks.** Psychological studies of transfer, where subjects are taught a skill and then are expected to automatically transfer that learning to a different domain, show that abilities generally don't transfer from one intelligence to another. For example, becoming a better reader will not necessarily make one a better math student, or learning to kick a soccer ball will not necessarily make it easier to paint a picture or relate well to another person. This general lack of transfer suggests the relative autonomy of each of the eight intelligences.

- **Potential Isolation by Brain Damage.** Disease or injury to certain areas of the brain appears to selectively impair specific intelligences while leaving the others intact. For example, an injury to Broca's area in the left frontal lobe of the brain can devastate a person's ability to speak or read, but that individual will often be able to paint, hum a tune, skate, or smile at another person because these functions are associated with unimpaired areas of the brain. However, an individual with damage to the right temporal lobe may lose the ability to carry a tune while retaining the ability to speak, read, and write. Roughly speaking, here are major areas of the brain that are associated with each of the eight intelligences:
  - *Linguistic:* left temporal and frontal lobes
  - *Logical-mathematical:* left frontal and right parietal lobes
  - *Spatial:* occipital and parietal regions (especially of right hemisphere)
  - *Bodily-kinesthetic:* cerebellum, basal ganglia, motor cortex
  - *Musical:* right temporal lobe
  - *Interpersonal:* frontal lobes, temporal lobe (especially right hemisphere), limbic system
  - *Intrapersonal:* frontal lobes, parietal lobes, limbic system
  - *Naturalist:* left parietal lobe (important for discriminating "living" from "nonliving things")

This last criterion showing how the eight intelligences correspond to different areas of the brain is of particular importance for us as we next look at the experience of reading and writing, and how these activities are mediated by neurological events in the brain.

Literacy Is a Whole-Brain Activity

It seems clear from the above survey of the eight intelligences that reading and writing are *linguistic* activities. The particular symbols used in reading and writing—in this case, the 26 letters of the English alphabet—are limited to this one intelligence. In addition, we tend to associate the activities of poets, playwrights, novelists, hyperlexic savants, and bookworms almost exclusively with linguistic intelligence. Certain distinctive brain structures, particularly in the left hemisphere for most people, are particularly important when it comes to the processing of the phonological, semantic, and syntactic aspects of words. In sum, there are strong reasons for literacy to be regarded as part and parcel of linguistic intelligence. Having said this, however, I'd like to argue that when we look at how the brain processes the actual *experience* of reading and writing, we can begin to see how *all* of the eight intelligences have important parts to play.

To illustrate, let's examine what happens in the brain during the simple act of speaking a printed word (see Figure 1.1). First the human eye must *see* the word on the page. This sensation is first registered by the primary visual area in the occipital lobe (the seat of spatial intelligence). After the word is seen in the primary visual area, it is then relayed to the angular gyrus (a "gyrus" is the crest of a single convolution in the neocortex), at the junction of the temporal, parietal, and occipital lobes of the brain. I like to think of the angular gyrus as the region of the brain that most reflects the idea of multiple intelligences' relationship to literacy because it is here, at the crossroads of three different lobes, that many different types of information are brought together or associated with each other in creating linguistic information, including visual-spatial configurations, musical and oral sounds, and even physical sensations. Recent research has suggested that individuals who have difficulty reading and writing often have significant disruption in this particular area of the brain (Horwitz, Rumsey, & Donohue, 1998). In the nearby region of Wernicke's area all of this information is synthesized in such a way that it can be understood in

Figure 1.1

Speaking a Written Word

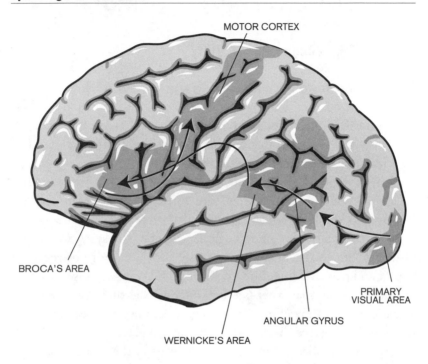

a *meaningful way* (i.e., semantically encoded). From there, it is transmitted via a bundle of nerve fibers called the *arcuate fasciculus* to Broca's area in the lower left frontal lobe, where it is logically encoded in a grammatical system, and a program is prepared to evoke articulation, and then supplied to the motor cortex, which in turn drives the muscles of the lips, tongue, and larynx to speak the actual word (Geschwind, 1979). Here then we see the involvement of several intelligences, including linguistic, logical-mathematical, spatial, and bodily-kinesthetic, in this simple act of speaking a printed word.

While the above scenario took place in the *left* hemisphere of the brain, there is increasing evidence that reading and writing involve significant use of the *right* hemisphere as well. Studies suggest, for example, that the right hemisphere is activated when subjects read words that are anxiety-provoking or emotionally charged (Van Strien, Stolk, & Zuiker, 1995). The right hemisphere also appears to be involved in semantic decisions during the reading and writing process, especially when the reader is in the initial stages of deciding among a range of possible words (Coney & Evans, 2000). In addition, the right hemisphere appears to take information that has been initially processed by the left hemisphere and uses it in the course of comprehending text (Coney, 1998). There are also subcortical structures involved in the process of reading, including the cerebellum, which has been previously linked to bodily-kinesthetic functions, and also areas of the limbic system that become activated while experiencing emotions during the process of reading (Fulbright et al., 1999; Simpson, Snyder, Gusnard, & Raichle, 2001). Unfortunately, we are still in the infancy of brain scan research regarding reading and writing activities, and too many studies are still based on a very limited context of literacy—for example, reading single words in an artificial laboratory setting rather than reading whole texts in a natural home or school setting (for recent criticisms of brain scan research and literacy, see Coles, 1998, 2000; Ferguson, 2002).

However, some of these newer brain studies (which will be reviewed in greater detail throughout the book) accord well with our understanding of the actual experiences involved in reading and writing. The person who reads and writes is doing far more than simply linguistically encoding data. She is also looking at the visual configuration of the letters. Thus, *spatial intelligence*—the intelligence of pictures and images—must first be brought to bear on the printed letters. Then she must match these visual images with sounds. In doing this, she must draw upon her wealth of knowledge concerning musical sounds (*musical intelligence*), nature sounds (*naturalist intelligence*), and the sounds of words (*linguistic intelligence*) in order to make the proper letter-sound correspondences. In addition, she brings in information from her body (*bodily-kinesthetic intelligence*) to ground these visual and auditory sensations into a structure of meaning. As we will see in Chapter 2, the physical body is integral to processing the shapes of letters and the meaning of words and text. Once she begins to organize the information into grammatical units, she draws upon deep intuitive syntactic structures that employ *logical-mathematical* transformations (see Chapter 5 for more information about this process). As she reads meaningful information, she may visualize what she reads (*spatial intelligence*), experience herself actively engaged in a physical way in the text (*bodily-kinesthetic intelligence*), have emotional reactions to the material (*intrapersonal intelligence*), attempt to guess what the author or characters intend or believe (*interpersonal intelligence*), and think critically and logically about what she is reading *(logical-mathematical intelligence)*. She may decide to take action as a result of her reading and writing, either in a physical way *(bodily-kinesthetic intelligence)* or perhaps within some larger social context *(interpersonal intelligence)*. In each of these cases, our reader is bringing to bear different intelligences upon the multilayered processes of reading and writing.

When we begin to think of literacy as involving *all* of the intelligences it becomes easier to understand the variety of ways in which literacy itself is learned and practiced. We know from the literature on individuals who have difficulty reading and writing that their difficulties are not all the same. Some students have particular problems with the visual configurations of letters (sometimes this is referred to as *dyseidetic dyslexia*), while others encounter difficulties primarily with the sounds of language *(dysphonetic dyslexia)*. Other students can decode individual words but encounter obstacles in comprehending whole text. Some individuals have problems primarily with the underlying grammatical-logical structures of sentences. Others have difficulties visualizing what they have read, or understanding what the author's intent may be.

By the same token, people actually learn to read in many different ways. For decades, many people learned to read with the old "look-say" *Dick and Jane* method. But it took a writer like Rudolf Flesch to point out that many students were being left out of this approach. As he indicated, some students need to learn to read by mastering the sounds or phonemes of language and their correspondences to the visual letters. Other students, however, have had difficulty with a decontextualized phonetic approach to reading and seem to do better with a method that emphasized real literature and natural contexts for reading and writing. Still other students thrive when other features are included in a reading and writing program, for example, involvement of the body, the use of the hands, a focus on color, an emphasis on the unique social milieu of the learner, the insertion of a particular component of great interest to the student such as animals, sports, or superheroes, or factors related to a student's individual learning style (see for example, Carbo, Dunn, & Dunn, 1986). As MIT linguist Steven Pinker points out, "it would not be surprising if language subcenters are idiosyncratically tangled or scattered over the cortex" (Pinker, 1994, p. 315). Such wide variations among learners suggest that instead of pitting one literacy method against another we need to discover how a student's unique brain is wired for reading and writing and then use a range of approaches that matches his or her "literacy style." It is for such a purpose that this book has been written.

While I will cite many studies that have focused on the breakdown of the capacity to read or write in individuals who have been described as "dyslexic," "learning disabled," or "reading disabled," the overall emphasis of the book is not on what's "wrong," but rather what's *right* with a student's reading and writing capacities. In fact, when I use labels such as "LD," "ADHD," and the like, I generally put them in quotation marks or otherwise qualify them, because of my belief that they are labels externally imposed within a specific social milieu (for more information, see Armstrong, 1997, 2000a).

Several years ago, a study on reading published in the *New England Journal of Medicine* received significant national attention by suggesting that individuals described as dyslexic were not part of a special species of learner separate from normal readers, but rather, that they represented the low end of a continuum of reading ability found in the rest of the population (Shaywitz, et al., 1992). I'd like to suggest that this continuum stretches from the nonreader all the way up to Shakespeare, and that every one of us falls somewhere along this spectrum. Instead of taking a "half-empty glass" perspective in thinking that everybody has a certain amount of reading disability in them, I prefer to take the "half-full glass" point of view in suggesting that even the student who has just written her first words is already on the road to writing like Shakespeare. And the fact is, there are multiple pathways to the highest peaks of literacy as we will see in the next eight chapters of this book. The biggest issue for educators to resolve regarding the Literacy Lion shouldn't be whether whole language or phonics is the best way to teach reading, or whether to focus on punctuation or creativity in writing, or whether we should teach students spelling skills or let them invent their own words. The biggest question is whether we as educators are going to teach literacy skills in such a way that the words lie dead there on the page for so many students, or, conversely, whether we're going to take positive steps toward the ultimate goal of *making the words come alive for all students.* I invite you to choose the second option, and, for the rest of this book join me in an adventure through the multiple intelligences of reading and writing.

For Further Study

- Research the history of "The Reading Wars" (and related "Writing Wars" and "Spelling Wars") since the 1950s, examining points of difference and areas of agreement.

- Stay current with the latest brain research in the fields of reading and writing, paying special attention to studies that link the right hemisphere and the limbic system and other subcortical areas of the brain to literacy (hint: use MEDLINE on the Internet as a key data source).

- Survey the literature on the applications of multiple intelligences theory to literacy. Read Howard Gardner's book *Frames of Mind* and other books on multiple intelligences, and make your own connections between MI theory and literacy acquisition.

- Examine the reading, writing, and spelling programs being used in your own educational setting and note which intelligences (besides linguistic) are being addressed in them.

2

Coming to Grips with the Musculature of Words

Words have power, they have *muscle*. Think of the toddler who has discovered a new word: "up!" That word has an almost magical quality for the child, because by merely saying it she can accomplish all sorts of physical actions. She can get mommy to come and pick her up and set her in a chair for a delicious dinner, she can be swooped up and given a big hug from daddy, or she can be put on big brother's shoulders and taken on a grand tour of the neighborhood. Never in a million years could she accomplish these things through her own meager physical efforts. But a single word does the trick. "Up!" has *muscle*.

Words have deep connections to the human musculature. Scientists believe that language emerged, at least in part, from the physical movements of primates and early humans: their gestures, facial expressions, postures, and other gross and subtle motor actions (see, for example, Varney, 2002). Interestingly, area F5 of the brain of monkeys, which is associated with the making of intentional physical movements, is considered analogous to Broca's area, one of the most important linguistic brain structures in human beings (Motluk, 2001).

In ways that are still too little understood, certain motor movements that functioned as communicative signs between humans over time became increasingly specialized in the vocal cords and other speech-producing areas of the body and brain. As one researcher noted: "The origin and evolution of language was the result of a transfer of motor patterning from that controlling bodily movement generally to the articulatory organs" (Allott, 2000). Another expert was even more blunt: "Linguistic structure may emerge from, and may even be viewed as, a special case of motoric structure, the structure of action" (Studdert-Kennedy, 1983). Similarly, our ability to *internally* operate on words and syntax as mental thought may have emerged from our capacity to manipulate physical objects. As San Francisco neurologist Frank Wilson writes: "Words that were originally object attributes come increasingly to be manipulated and combined, just as real objects are manipulated and combined by the child" (Wilson, 1998, p. 193).

There is growing evidence from brain research pointing to a strong neurological basis for this link between physical movement and language and literacy. Neuroscientists, of course, have known for quite a while that the motor cortex is an important part of the language process, being responsible for the movement of the muscles of the tongue, mouth, and throat in order to produce audible speech sounds (Geschwind, 1979). However, more recently, with the emergence of neuroimaging technologies and new genetic techniques, there has been increasing evidence that language and literacy are also linked to other areas of the brain that have traditionally been seen as the locus of bodily-kinesthetic capacities. A study published in the medical journal *Nature* described the discovery of a specific gene tied to a particular set of language disorders; this gene is involved in the development of the basal ganglia, a set of brain structures that are crucial for regulating motor movements (Wade, 2001). In addition, over the past few years, researchers have been focusing on the cerebellum, that "ancient brain" at the base of the skull responsible for coordinating complex physical movements in three-dimensional space, as an important contributor to language capacity. This influence may extend beyond oral language to reading skills. Recently, NASA scientists have noted that astronauts who had experienced prolonged periods of weightlessness in space—creating disturbances of the cerebellum—sometimes suffered from mild dyslexia on returning to earth conditions (Meikle, 2001). A recent neuroimaging study using functional MRI supported this cerebellum-reading link in its findings of cerebellar activation while subjects engaged in several reading tasks that required orthographic, phono-logic, and semantic skills (Fulbright, et al., 1999; see also, Nicolson & Fawcett, 1999).

Further evidence for the connection of literacy to the physical body can be seen by examining the development of language historically, and in particular, the history of the English language. The Middle English word for "remorse" was originally "agonbite," an acutely kinesthetic way of rendering the sense of guilt (literally, "agony biting one's insides"). Shakespeare's works are filled with kinesthetic images and expressions. For example, when Macbeth is trying to decide whether or not to kill Duncan, the king of Scotland, he says: "I have no spur to prick the sides of my intent, but only vaulting ambition, which o'er-leaps itself and falls on th'other side" (*Macbeth*, Act 1, Scene 7). Today's language is not nearly so rich with bodily sensations and movements, but if we engage in a bit of lexical archeology, we can see in many highly abstract words the origins of physical activity. The word "error" for example, goes back to the Latin for "to wander" (it's related to the French word "errant"). The word "person" goes back to the Latin word "persona," meaning mask, performer, or actor. Even the word "process" is based upon a Latin word meaning "to proceed."

We can also see how literacy emerged from the body by examining the development of print historically. Before the invention of the print-ing press in the 15th century, all manuscripts were written down *by hand*. That meant that the process of reading was intimately inter-twined with the intensive manual labor of calligraphy. Medieval students sat at their places in medieval universities and laboriously transcribed their teachers' lectures (the word lecture comes from the Latin word *legere*, "to read"). The act of reading itself often involved touch-ing the words as one read, speaking the words out loud, and putting one's whole physical and mental energy into the work of understanding and comprehending. Clerical scholar Dom Jean LeClercq observed: "When *legere* and *lectio* [to read] are used without further explanation, they mean an activity which, like chant and writing, requires the participation of the whole body and the whole mind. Doctors of ancient times used to recommend reading to their patients as a physical exercise on an equal level with walking, running or ball-playing"

(McLuan, 1965, p. 89). Marshall McLuan refers to the pre-Gutenberg manuscripts of medieval and classic times as "highly textural and tactile." Note the relationship between the linguistic word "text" and the kinesthetic word "texture"; the word "Textura" was actually a name used for Gothic lettering (McLuan, 1965, p. 83).

Another way to understand the bodily-kinesthetic foundations of literacy is by inquiring into the inner worlds of those individuals who excel in the realm of the printed word—in other words, writers. More than a few of them reveal idiosyncratic ways in which hands-on and physical sensations play a major part in their creative process. The philosopher and psychologist William James explained his own method of letter recall as a tactile experience: "I myself am a very poor visualizer, and find that I can seldom call to mind even a single letter of the alphabet in purely retinal terms. I must trace the letter by running my mental eye over its contour in order that the image of it shall leave any distinctness at all" (James, 1910, p. 61). The British writer A. E. Housman explained his own process in writing poetry quite literally as getting the goosebumps: "Experience has taught me, when I am shaving of a morning, to keep watch over my thoughts, because, if a line of poetry strays into my memory, my skin bristles so that the razor ceases to act. This particular symptom is accompanied by a shiver down the spine; there is another which consists in a constriction of the throat, and a precipitation of water to the eyes; and there is a third which I can only describe by borrowing a phrase from one of Keats's last letters, where he says, speaking of Fanny Brawne, 'everything that reminds me of her goes through me like a spear.' The seat of this sensation is the pit of the stomach" (Ghiselin, 1960, p. 90).

I should add here, parenthetically, that my own work as a writer bears out the kinesthetic experience: I know that I am writing at or near my best when I get a particular sensation deep in my belly. I also have a peculiar sense of the text that appears on the computer screen as I write, as a thicket of words with a definite textural feeling: the better the text, the thicker the feeling; the more superficial the text, the thinner the physical sensation that I have in my body. Finally, let me include the childhood reminiscence of the great American writer Eudora Welty: "At around age six, perhaps, I was standing by myself in our front yard waiting for supper, just at that hour in a late summer day when the sun is already below the horizon and the risen full moon in the visible sky stops being chalky and begins to take on light. There comes a moment, and I saw it then, when the moon goes from flat to round. For the first time it met my eyes as a globe. The word 'moon' came into my mouth as though fed to me out of a silver spoon" (Angell, 2001). For young children, words have a physical reality. In their eyes, the word "hit" can actually hurt someone (Piaget, 1975).

This last experience brings us back to the importance that the body has in the first literacy experiences of young children. When we observe pre-literacy or emerging literacy in early childhood, we see it expressed in large motor movements: the child who is busy "reading" a book will often make a big show of turning the pages, opening the mouth wide to speak, moving the head back and forth, and rocking back and forth. For the emergent reader, reading is not the quiet passive experience of sitting stone cold still in a chair with eyes fixed rigidly on a page. Reading is a physical performance! Emergent *writing* is often even more physical, with the young child sometimes using the writing implement quite literally as a "tool" to dig meaning into the surface of the page. In the emerging literate scrawlings of the young child, the boundaries between etching, sculpting, drawing, and writing seem to disappear, as they also did in a highly refined and articulated way in the creative work of William Blake (Bentley, 2001).

The above material from brain research, the history of the English language, early childhood development, and the creative process of writers suggests that literacy programs need to address in some significant way the role that the physical body has in reading and writing. What follows are suggestions for how the fuller integration of the body into a comprehensive literacy program might proceed.

Making Letters and Sounds That Crawl, Dance, and Jump

Recent research in the gestural equivalence of language has attempted to create direct correspondences between specific phonemes and discrete gestures (Allott, 2000). Along these lines, existing educational programs have made efforts to link letters or sounds with particular body movements, including educational eurythmy (Steiner, 1983) and Zoo-phonics (Atterman, 1997), or have linked the physical act of producing specific lip, mouth, and tongue patterns with individual phonemes. See, for example, the Lindamood-Bell program (Howard, 1982). Although there are obvious and significant differences in the way these programs work, at a deeper level they share the belief that providing a motoric equivalent to a letter shape or a speech sound will give the beginning reader a much better chance of remembering sound-symbol relationships. As such, any educator can create a "physical phonics" program, simply by taking the roughly 44 phonemes in the English language and developing a unique gesture, posture, or physical movement for each one. For example, the long *e* sound might be represented as the hands moving away from each other as if pulling taffy, while the long *o* sound might involve bringing the extended arms upwards above the head in a rounded fashion as if creating a large circle. If every beginning reader were taught 44 separate physical actions that corresponded to the 44 phonemes, they could then draw upon this motor memory bank in helping to recall the specific sound-symbol pattern that each movement represents. In fact, it might be preferred that the teacher use her own creativity to come up with these movements, or draw upon the innovation of the learners themselves to generate this kinesthetic vocabulary.

Similarly, for help in learning the visual patterns of letters, educators since Montessori have used physical and tactile methods, especially in the field of special education (e.g., Fernald, 1988). Examples of this type of approach include

- Tracing letter shapes in the air, or on the desk or table.
- Tracing letter shapes cut out from textural material (e.g., sandpaper, silk).
- Making letter shapes from pipe cleaners, clay, or other malleable material.
- Making letter shapes with finger paint, chocolate pudding, whipped cream, or some other messy and fun medium.
- Manipulating block letter shapes.
- Drawing letter shapes in dirt, sand, or other impressionable material.
- Writing letter shapes with large body movements using chalk on a large pavement surface (such as the school playground).
- Creating letter shapes with atypical writing implements such as a paintbrush, a squirt gun, or a flashlight in the dark.

There really is no end to developing innovative ways for the visual shapes of letters to be tied to their physical "feel." One teacher, for example, put letter shapes in waterproof tape on the bottom of a swimming pool and asked a student who had significant difficulty learning the alphabet to *swim* the letter shapes. I have often thought that if every schoolyard had a playground that included 26 giant alphabet sculptures for kids to climb on and crawl under and around and through, there would be no need to teach the alphabet at all inside the classroom.

Getting Physical with Words

Educators can also use many of the above techniques as the beginning reader starts to put letters together into meaningful combinations, or words. And I employ the active voice here intentionally, because the student should be *actively* involved in constructing these meaningful units of letters. Here are some other ways they can do this:

- Using an alphabet stamp set to create words.
- Building words as sculpture using clay, wood, or other plastic materials. Here the word exists as an art form, in the fashion of a sculptor such as Robert Indiana (see Janson, 1969, p. 542).
- Carving words into wood or other malleable materials.
- Making words from string, wire, twine, thread, chains, or other solid material that mimics the line of a pen or pencil (students can paste these on a surface permanently, or manually reshape them for each new word).

Similarly, in learning the *spelling* patterns of words, there are a number of activities that actively use manipulatives or creative body movements in remembering specific word orders or consonant-vowel patterns (Barsch, 1974). For example:

- Spell the word out loud while bouncing a ball (or skipping rope) one time for each successive letter.
- Spell the word out loud while standing up whenever a consonant appears, and sitting down whenever a vowel appears (any

other two physical movements could be substituted for standing and sitting).

- Spell the word using a series of pantomimed gestures representing the letters of the word (have students develop their own unique pantomimes for each letter of the alphabet—essentially designing an "alpha-betics" exercise program).

- Spell the word using alphabet blocks or plastic materials.

- Spell the word using blue chips (for vowels) and red chips (for consonants) (or substitute any other two materials).

While actively engaged in physically creating words, students should also be expressing their *meanings* as well. The simplest and most direct way of doing this is by acting out the word in some way. The old parlor game "charades" is probably the best example of an activity that promotes kinesthetic expression of word meanings. Students who have a special dramatic flair, yet who do poorly with traditional reading approaches, are most likely to benefit from this type of approach, yet all kids will have fun learning sight words, or vocabulary words, by pantomiming or dramatizing them. I've talked with high school educators who have had students photograph some of the best examples of these dramatized word meanings. For example, one student illustrated the meaning of the word "abashed" with a picture of a student with his trousers pulled down to his knees, revealing only his multi-colored boxer shorts! These word meanings can also be acted out and then videotaped. How refreshing to have this week's list of sight words or vocabulary words presented as a film of dramatic scenes, rather than a boring list of definitions in a workbook.

Creating Sentences That Are (Literally) Moving

I believe that it was Maria Montessori's teachings that first suggested to me the importance of linking reading directly to action. Too often, beginning reading students read simple sentences out loud, and then just leave them there dead on the page in an unfulfilled state. Montessori's great innovation was to have students read a sentence on a slip of paper. and then carry out the activity or action that it represented. Montessori was, of course, an exceedingly practical educator, and so it made sense for her to include sentences that involved specific useful tasks such as "Water the plants at the back of the room," or "Pick up the book that has fallen on the floor." Students might actually enjoy the process of composing their own practical sentences. This kind of activity tells them, from the very beginning of their experience with literacy, that words have the power of action.

I want to highlight the point that students should be actively *writing* the sentences that they read. If you want to think of it in this way, *writing is actually just a highly kinesthetic way of reading*, and so you might want to consider it as an excellent strategy for helping the beginning reader master the code. Remember what I said at the beginning of this chapter about the historical origins of literacy: before the printing press, all reading material had to be written down by hand. So when the first meaningful sentences that a student learns to read are those he has inscribed himself with his own hand, there is a direct physical connection to the words and their meaning from the very beginning. Here are some other ways to get physically involved in the composition of simple sentences:

- Have the student create a hanging mobile with each word of a sentence on a card or other piece of material.

- Put the words of a sentence on index cards, or better yet, on less academic material (such as blocks, or color swatches) and have the student create the sentence by manipulating the materials. If you really want to get creative, teach the student how to juggle with three balls. Then have the student put a word on each ball to make a three-word sentence that she can say as she juggles the balls in order!

- Use magnetic words (these are often sold at bookstores near the cash registers) on a metallic surface so that the student can create sentences.

- Inscribe the words of a sentence on pieces of construction paper, and then tape them to the floor. Have the student speak the sentence while stepping on each successive word, in a linguistic version of the games hopscotch or Twister.

Putting the Texture Back into Text

A few years back I was addressing the National Family Literacy Association at a convention in Louisville, Kentucky, and they had just had a celebration the night before where tens of thousands of pieces of confetti, each one inscribed with a word, had been released and still lay on the floor waiting to be picked up the morning after. I whimsically suggested to the group that they might consider trying to reconstruct the novel *Gone with the Wind* from the scattered pieces. Once we begin working with blocks of text, even texts much shorter than Margaret Mitchell's novel, it becomes harder and more time consuming to use many of the technique listed in the previous section. However, I should point out that if a student is working with short paragraphs, it's still possible to use manipulatives to put the text together, or even to inscribe the paragraph in chalk on a large surface of pavement, and then have the students *walk* the paragraph as they read it. In fact, it would be wonderful to have in each school in the country a dedicated space where a large body of text (perhaps a famous poem, or a selection from an inspirational speech, or a passage from a descriptive short story) is colorfully and texturally inscribed on the floor, so that students could regularly take time to physically stroll across the text while reading it. (Perhaps such a text could be changed regularly, so that new reading material would always be available for students to walk, crawl, or run across.)

Beyond such whimsical and somewhat extraordinary suggestions for putting the "texture" back into "text," the greater part of the bodily-kinesthetic focus on text should be on helping students explore, understand, and express the text's meaning in physical ways. I've often suggested to educators that if, after reading a story, teachers would simply have students quickly role-play the material that they have just read, reading comprehension levels would increase rapidly for many students, particularly for many of those students who have been labeled as having attention deficit hyperactivity disorder or learning disabilities (Armstrong, 1997, 1999b, 2000b). There are many ways to work with specific reading comprehension skills through drama, role-play, or pantomime. For example, students might be asked to give the main idea of a passage by providing a "freeze frame" montage (students assemble themselves in a way that captures the theme), which can then be photographed or videotaped and compared with other groups' physical conceptions of the main idea. Or, on an individual basis, a student might be given a lump of clay, some art supplies, or other plastic materials, and asked to express the main idea through a three-dimensional construction. To help students understand character development in a story, they might be invited to work out a pantomime that expresses the stages a particular character goes through in facing the challenges or conflicts of the story. What we're asking students to do is think through material in the text *through their bodies*, instead of simply requiring them to sit still at their desks and do all the thinking invisibly.

A particularly effective way to engage students is by having them read the material and act it out *simultaneously*. Plays are, of course, the best medium for doing this. I remember attending a high school Shakespeare class at an international school in England where the students were standing in the classroom, each with a play in hand, reading and interacting with each other, while the teacher went around to each "reader/actor" helping them get into the physical feeling of their character. At one point, the teacher encouraged a student to actually *slap* the script of another student in order to embody the enmity felt by the one character toward the other. Little physical cues like this can have an immense impact upon a student's involvement in a text.

I should point out, however, that an educator can still help students comprehend text using bodily-kinesthetic intelligence without ever even having students leave their desks. This can be accomplished by asking students to explore the meanings of text through their own internal kinesthetic imagery. Kinesthetic imagery refers to inner imagery that represents physical movement, bodily sensations, and tactile impressions (Houston, 1982). A few preliminary exercises can prepare students to understand this form of imagery: have them imagine walking down a road that's been freshly paved with tar (and feeling the imaginary stickiness on their imaginary feet), or basking in the sun (and feeling the imaginary warmth on their imaginary skin), or lifting a heavy weight (and feeling the strain in their imaginary muscles). Tell them that in addition to having a physical body, they also have an imaginary kinesthetic body. Have them raise their actual left arm in the air and put it down again. Then, have them raise and lower their "kinesthetic arm" (their imaginary left arm) without putting their real physical arm in the air. These kinds of exercises prepare them to understand what is meant by kinesthetic imagery. Then, after reading a text, have the students experience the action of the text (if it is a narrative) by closing their eyes and imagining themselves in the story. If a character in the story is swimming, have the students imagine *themselves* swimming, focusing on the sensations they have in their bodies, on their skin, and so on. If a character has just eaten an ice cream cone, have the students feel the coldness on their lips and in their throat, and the sweetness and taste of the ice cream, and the crunchiness of the cone.

Some students (especially younger ones) will easily adapt to this kind of approach, and will even outwardly make the actions of licking the ice cream, smacking their lips, and so forth. Other students (such as high school level and adult learners) may have difficulty getting involved in the imagery at first, and may actually need help in accessing the imagery by doing the action outwardly. For example, if a character in a story has just yawned, you might have the students actually yawn themselves as a prompt to identify with the action of the character.

Teachers should particularly identify text where the author has emphasized the use of kinesthetic imagery in the choice of words, metaphors, phrases, and narrative devices. I've already mentioned above how often this occurs in the works of our greatest English writer, William Shakespeare. Pick up virtually any play at random, open a page, and you will find a kinesthetic metaphor. For example, in *Henry V*, the French Duke of Orleans insults the English army by saying: "Foolish curs, that run winking into the mouth of a Russian bear and have their heads crushed like rotten apples" (Act 3, Scene 7). Or, in *Julius Caesar*, Antony comments in the wake of Caesar's assassination: "O pardon me, thou bleeding piece of earth, that I am meek and gentle with these butchers" (Act 3, Scene 1). Even the names Shakespeare uses for his characters are often kinesthetic, especially his comic figures (for example, in *A Midsummer Night's Dream*: Nick Bottom, Tom Snout, Robin Starveling). A more contemporary example, James Joyce's *Ulysses* (the work considered by many critics to be the greatest English-language novel of the 20th century) has an entire chapter dedicated to the body, where the narrative action mimics the peristalsis action of the intestines (with many fitful stops and starts). These works are the touchstones of English language literacy. While few authors reach this height, educators should always be on the lookout in any text for the possibility that kinesthetic imagery may be present. And once kinesthetic imagery has been located in a text, consider accentuating the author's imagery by having students act out the images in the classroom. For example, when Hamlet says in his famous "To be, or not to be" speech, "Whether 'tis nobler in the mind to suffer the slings and arrows of outrageous fortune . . . " (*Hamlet*, Act 3, Scene 1), students might stand up and briefly act out the gestures involved in being hit with arrows or stones from a slingshot. Or, in a simpler story, if an author writes: "He walked as if with a chip on his shoulder," a teacher might give students game chips and ask them to put the chips on their shoulders and walk around the classroom, and then discuss the meaning of the expression and its significance in the context of the story.

Bodily-Kinesthetic Books and Other Literacy Materials

When selecting books and other literacy materials for highly bodily-kinesthetic learners, especially for those who are intimidated by books, it's important to keep in mind that books can involve much more than words; increasingly, nontraditional books that combine words with tactile, physical, or kinesthetic possibilities are being published. I'd like to highlight two publishers in particular, Klutz Press, 455 Portage Ave., Palo Alto, CA 94306, 650-857-0888, klutz-press@aol.com or http://www.klutz.com, and Workman Publishing Company, 708 Broadway, New York, NY 10003-9555, 212-254-5900, info@workman.com. Many of the books sold by these two publishers include attached materials that involve bodily movement or hands-on exploration. For example, a book on juggling is packaged with juggling balls, a book on jump rope rhymes includes a jump rope, and a book on creating with clay comes packaged with the actual clay. These books are exciting because they exemplify a direct relationship between reading and *doing*. By actively exploring the materials, students become interested in what's inside the book, which leads to more informed use of the materials in a positive cycle of mutual reinforcement.

Other publishers have gone even further by creating books that actually come apart and can be reconstructed into something useful or instructive—for example, creating a working clock or a medieval castle from the materials of the book. For very young children, touch-and-feel books provide an immediate tactile experience along with the words, and scratch-and-sniff books give tactile and olfactory stimulation. For upper elementary to adult learners, any how-to book, even if devoid of hands-on features, nevertheless promotes active exploration and should be considered part of any bodily-kinesthetic library. Also, look at selecting books for their tactile and physical qualities. Some books consist of paper with a rougher or smoother "feel" than average, or have more deeply inscribed print that readers can touch as they read along. Other books, in their largeness or smallness, or unusual shape, make reading and manipulating the book a unique physical event. Finally, the ultimate kinesthetic experience is to engage students in making their own books from scratch, including making the paper, the ink, and the bindings, and then doing their own calligraphy on the pages.

Bodily-Kinesthetic Literacy Styles

Back in the 1970s, when I was just starting out in teaching, I became familiar with a literacy program called *Modern Reading* that was being used with so-called "at risk" boys who today we would label ADHD and perhaps also conduct disordered (von Hilshiemer, 1970). What interested me about this program was that it was based on teaching reading in a fast-paced style (individual reading sessions with the instructor lasted only a minute or two) and it let the students chew gum while reading comics independently in groups lying on the floor among soft pillows. Now, as I look back on this long-defunct program, I realize that it was a product of the '60s counterculture and is not likely to be replicated soon in any of today's school systems. And yet, I see in this program something admirable, and that is its recognition of the need to match literacy acquisition with the tempo and style of the students. It was a hyperactive program for hyperactive students! This realization suggests something more fundamental to me, and that is that we need to consider the broader "literacy styles" of students in helping them learn to read and write. And it seems to me that the traditional image we have of literacy acquisition—that of a student sitting at a desk quietly turning pages or writing with a pen or pencil—does not really work for the highly bodily-kinesthetic student. Instead, we need to consider ways in which we can, as educators, reconceptualize the processes of reading and writing to consider the needs of students who are movers, builders, touchers, and squirmers. What this means, in part, is that we need to discard the traditional image of the silent, motionless reader or writer and envision other, more tactile and mobile ways in which literacy can be achieved and practiced. Here are some suggestions:

- Let students read standing up, lying down, or in some other posture that allows them to feel comfortable (and provide a corresponding learning environment where this can be achieved, such as a cozy reading area with pillows and soft carpeting). This practice should apply not just to young children, but also to older learners as well (where comfortable sofas or easy chairs may be more appropriate).

- Give students opportunities to move and read at the same time. For example, students could walk while they read in a "reading and moving" space. (I should point out that the image of a scholar reading while walking around was quite predominant in the 18th and 19th centuries, and numerous instances of this can be found in the literature of the time.) For older students and adult learners, suggest the possibility of reading while on an exercise bike or other fitness machine (many models now include a holder for books, newspapers, and magazines).

- Allow students to use their hands and fingers while they read. Speed-reading programs have long used finger movements as a way to keep the eye moving at a fast rate. Touching the words that one reads increases the kinesthetic connection to the material (remember what I said above about the historical origins of reading as a *tactile* experience).

- Whenever possible, let students *write* in the books that they read and in other ways interact manually with their books. I'm not talking here of workbooks that are meant to be written in, but rather about physical engagement with real books and other literacy materials. When a student can interact directly and physically with the book, writing in the margins, making notations, dog-earing special pages, manipulating bookmarks, and putting sticky notes on favorite passages, for example, there is a real sense of kinesthetic involvement with a book. A well-worn book (which should be seen as one of the most admirable signs of literacy) is like a well-worn sofa or couch, displaying hours, days, or years of direct physical contact.

- Allow students to use pens, pencils, and other writing implements that provide tactile stimulation. Some writing implements come with special grips or shapes that fit especially well in the hand or that feel good to the touch. A graphite pencil provides a certain vibration on the surface of a piece of paper that is very different from that of a ballpoint pen or a fountain pen, and these differences may be important to the highly kinesthetic learner. Also, as with reading, let students use paper for writing that has interesting textures and surfaces.

- Let students precede or follow their reading and writing with physical exercises designed to help them relax, center, or just get the jiggles out of their system. These exercises can include progressive relaxation, educational kinesiology or Brain-Gym activities (Dennison & Dennison, 1994; Hannaford, 1995), yoga, stretching, aerobics, calisthenics, or any other activity that may help the highly physical learner. Some students may be more amenable to learning to read or write if they've just come from a physical education class or have been involved in a sport of some kind.

For Further Study

I hope that the suggestions provided in this chapter will spur further research and application of bodily-kinesthetic intelligence to literacy issues. Here are some suggestions for getting started right away:

- Create a "body-phonics" program by linking each of the 44 phonemes of the English language (or those specific phonemes that students have greatest difficulty with) to a specific physical movement, posture, or gesture.

- Design an area of the learning environment that allows students to read and move, or write and move, at the same time.

- Look over the text material that you are currently using in your program and identify specific examples of kinesthetic imagery used by the author that you can highlight and work with in your lessons.

- Take a list of "sight words" and have students create physical movements or freeze-frame postures that go along with each word meaning. Then photograph or videotape the list of word performances for future reference.

- Create a "bodily-kinesthetic library" of books for your students (including books that have hands-on attachments and books that can be manipulated or taken apart and put back together as three-dimensional structures).

- Develop five new spelling strategies that engage the whole body.

- Inscribe a piece of text on a large floor surface (indoors or outdoors), and then engage students in reading the text with their *feet*. Have them stop along the way to act out word meanings or dramatize the content of particular sections.

3

Seeing the Visual Basis of Literacy

When I was a young child, perhaps five years old, Wednesdays were always special days on TV. Every Wednesday, Pinky Lee (host of a children's show in the mid 1950s) would appear on screen with a large flip chart and draw on a sheet of paper one of the letters of the alphabet. Then he would proceed to turn it into a picture. One day, for example, he drew a huge *A* on the paper, and then went about putting a little chimney toward the top, a door at the bottom, and windows throughout. Suddenly, it was no longer an *A*, it was a house!

I just thought this was the most exciting thing I'd ever seen, and every week I tuned in to see what kind of new magic he was going to make with letters and pictures. I didn't know it at the time, but what Pinky was doing there on the television screen for millions of kids was uncovering, in his own fun-loving way, the deep connections between written symbols and visual imagery.

The Visual-Spatial Foundations of Words

Robinson (1995) points out that "the first written symbols are generally thought to have been pictograms, pictorial representations of concrete objects" (p. 11). We see examples of this in the pictographic writing of North American Indians. But Robinson goes on to say: "Essential to the development of full writing . . . was the discovery of the rebus principle. This was the radical idea that a pictographic symbol could be used for its phonetic value. Thus a drawing of an owl in Egyptian hieroglyphs could represent a consonantal sound with an inherent *m;* and in English a picture of a bee with a picture of a leaf might (if one were so minded) represent the word belief" (p. 12). All current written languages have emerged from this pictographic/rebus principle, although some languages—such as Chinese and the Kanji script of Japanese—have retained their connection to the picture world much more fully than other more phonological languages such as Finnish and English. Interestingly, one study suggested that in some cases it is easier teaching children identified as "reading disabled" to read visually based Chinese characters than more highly phonologically based English words, presumably because these students are more highly developed in visual-spatial intelligence than in linguistic-phonological processing (Rozin, Poritsky, and Sotsky, 1971).

However, as Pinky Lee showed, the English language itself is full of visual-spatial possibilities. The reading process begins in the brain when the eye sends information about the visual forms of the markings on the page to the visual cortex in the occipital lobes. Before these sensations have been relayed for processing as linguistic information by the angular gyrus and Wernicke's area, these marks are not viewed as phonological symbols, but rather as pictures on a par with any other kind of picture (hence, my joy at seeing letters treated as pictures on the Pinky Lee Show). One study of 1st graders indicated that students initially viewed the alphabet with the visual-spatial areas of the brain in the right hemisphere and only later, by 3rd grade, were regularly transferring this perception over to the language centers in the left hemisphere (Carmon, Nachshon, and Starinsky, 1976).

Visual processing also occurs once letters have been combined into words having semantic content. Hence, when the child reads the word *car*, for example, images of cars may flash before her inner eye, or she may visualize a forest or grove when the word *trees* appears on the written page. Even words that don't have concrete visual antecedents may evoke visual images in the reader. A look at some abstract words in the English language reveals shards of visual imagery in them. For example, the word *shipment* has the word *ship* in it, indicating that shipment once referred directly to maritime cargo. The adjective *outlandish* at one time referred to strangers or foreigners (literally, people who were from *outside of the land*). Many abstract English words also have visual origins from other languages. The word *calculate*, for example, comes from the Latin word *calculus*, meaning *pebble* (small stones were used in abacuses at that time). Even the word *idea* has a direct visual reference—it comes from the Greek *idein,* meaning *to see.*

Rudolf Arnheim (1969), professor emeritus of the psychology of art at Harvard University, suggests that behind every word is some kind of visual image. Arnheim pointed to early (American) psychologist Edward B. Titchener as an example of someone who produced strikingly precise visual imagery from even the most nonconcrete words:

> Titchener, after sitting on [a] platform behind "a somewhat emphatic lecturer, who made great use of the monosyllable 'but' had his 'feeling of but' associated ever afterward with 'a flashing picture of a bald crown, with a fringe of hair below, and a massive black shoulder, the whole passing swiftly down the visual field, from northwest to southeast'" (p. 111).

Titchener also associated the word *meaning* with "the blue-grey tip of a kind of scoop, which has a bit of yellow above it (probably a part of the handle), and which is just digging into a dark mass of what appears to be plastic material."

As readers begin to incorporate more and more words into their vocabulary and string them together into meaningful sentences and larger texts, their ability to access a rich landscape of imagery accordingly. One study of three well-known contemporary writers suggests a wide range of individual differences when it comes to creating visual imagery while reading texts (Esrock, 1986). The writer John Hawkes revealed a high level of visual imagery while reading: "I couldn't read without forming a visual image. I've never read any fiction so abstract that you wouldn't form a visual image. I've never read a fiction that doesn't have a landscape, doesn't create a world, some kind of space.

And we can see what's in it . . . at any moment, really, I'm in a totally constructed visual world" (p. 62). On the other hand, William Gass reports that he visualizes very little when reading nonfiction, and almost never when reading literature, while celebrated Mexican writer Carlos Fuentes is somewhere between the two, indicating that his visual imagery while reading requires a "verbal substratum" or it rapidly disintegrates. In other words, he limits his visual imagery to only what the text authorizes and goes no further with his imagination. A number of studies indicate that the use of visualization strategies assists readers in becoming more accomplished at comprehending text (Gambrell and Bales, 1986; Borduin, Borduin, and Manley, 1994; Rose, Parks, Androes, and McMahon, 2000), and provides writers with prewriting skills to enhance creativity (Wright, 1991; Tims and Williams, 1992).

Picturing Letters and Sounds

One of the educational implications of Pinky Lee's "letter of the week" demonstration is that letters and letter sounds should be introduced to children (and to adult learners) through pictorial methods. In fact, one such method was worked out over 80 years ago by German educator Rudolf Steiner (1976). Steiner advised that the alphabet be introduced to children through pictures and images that are imaginatively developed by the teachers themselves. In Waldorf schools based upon Steiner's teachings, the letter *S*, for example, may be introduced initially through the image of a snake. Students might hear a story about a snake, such as *Riki-Tiki-Tavi*, and create a play and make drawings from the story. Only after being fully immersed in the imagery of the story and images of snakes will the teacher put on the blackboard her own series of pictures of a snake that over time gradually evolves into the letter *S* (see Figure 3.1).

The sound-symbol correspondence is also part of the story, as the hissing sound of the snake gradually turns into the "sssss" sound of the *S* consonant. Similarly, the letter *M* may be introduced in the shape of a "mouth" and gradually assume the shape of an *M* (along with the sound that is made by the mouth when the lips are closed: "mmmm-mmm"). This approach to letter form and sound gradually moves

Figure 3.1

Gradual Evolution of a Snake into the Letter *S*

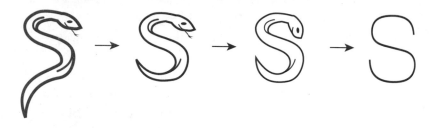

students from the world of imagery (and musicality) into the world of linguistic sounds and symbols. As such it represents a more gentle introduction to the alphabet than is the norm for many young kids who, coming into traditional classrooms, stare at the alphabet cards strung high up on the classroom walls, and feel the remoteness of these strange markings to their own imagery-rich lives. Because research suggests that many children who have reading and language difficulties excel in visual-spatial capacities (see, for example, Geschwind, 1982; West, 1997; Armstrong, 2000b), introducing letters as pictures may have particular relevance to those populations who are apt to experience reading difficulty with more traditional phonetic methods.

Another approach to sound-symbol correspondence that is visually based is Gattegno's Words in Color reading program (Gattegno, 1985), a program that was more popular in the 1960s and 1970s, but that is still available today (through Educational Solutions, 99 University Place, 2nd Floor, New York, NY 10003-4555; phone: 212-674-2988; e-mail: edusol99@aol.com). In Words in Color, each of the phonemes of the English language is assigned a particular color. As students begin to read simple words, they are able to sound out letters based upon their color-sound correspondence. Thus the *a* in *cat* will be a different color than the *a* in *car* because they have different sound values, while the same color will be used for the *f* in *fine* and the *ph* in *photo* because they have the same sound. Gradually, as students become accustomed to the letter-color-sound correspondences, the colors are removed and students proceed to read text in black and white. Some educators may object to this approach by questioning how a child can possibly remember and discriminate among more than 40 different colors. In response, one can point out that some children may find this task far easier than remembering and discriminating among over 40 different *sounds,* and that the use of color provides an additional source of priming to the highly visual child trying to identify different sound-symbol relationships. It is true that such an approach would likely create special difficulties and confusions for individuals who are color blind or who have difficulty discriminating between subtle shades of reds, blues, and other colors (and for these individuals, such an approach would obviously not be recommended). However, it does give one an appreciation for the fact that reading programs based heavily on auditory discrimination of the 44 phonemes of the English language may create obstacles that are just as great for those children who have particular difficulties discriminating sounds.

These two reading approaches (Steiner's and Gattegno's) point the way for educators to develop their own unique methods to help beginning readers learn the sound-symbol code in a highly visual-spatial way. For example, teachers might take the 44 phonemes of English and assign a color to each (as in the Gattegno program), or assign a unique picture symbol to each, or to particularly difficult phonemes. These visual symbols might be placed above the letter or letter combination to indicate the appropriate pronunciation (as in the use of diacritical marks). On a less systematic level, to assist in the learning of the alphabet, the visual form of each letter of the alphabet might be heightened through artistic elaboration. Teachers and kids can become their own Pinky Lees and create pictures from each of the letters. Teachers can select alphabets and alphabet books that are visually more interesting than the standard alphabet series that appear in many classrooms.

It should be remembered that before the introduction of the printing press, manuscript letters in the Middle Ages were often richly ornate and were viewed as works of art in themselves (calligraphy, of course, is an art form with a long history in many world traditions including Asian and Islamic cultures). In the West, even after the advent of the printing press, fonts were often quite visually complex. Only in recent times, with the mass publication of books and other texts, have letter fonts become more and more homogenized, with very little visually to discriminate between letters (see Logan, 1986). For example, there is very little visual difference between a **b** and a **d** other than directionality, which may not provide enough visual information for some beginning readers to see the difference. It remains for researchers to investigate whether this culturally based homogenization of print may be at least partly to blame for the reversal of letters occurring in students just beginning to read or write, or among those experiencing special reading and writing difficulties. In any case, teachers can accentuate the visual impact of letters by using art techniques as well as the word-processing features of computer software to create a variety of font types and sizes (along with the use of italics, underlining, bold, and color) to provide students with text that is visually compelling and interesting. Zentall and Kruczek (1988) suggest, in particular, that the use of color in letter formation may heighten the interest and attention of children labeled ADHD.

Turning Words into Works of Art

One of my favorite literacy experiences in middle childhood was reading *Mad Magazine*. A regular feature of *Mad* was to visually show the sense of different words by spatially transforming the words into their actual meaning. So, for example, the word *tall* would appear with very high letters, and the word *short* would be spelled with tiny letters. The cartoonists also played around with words pictorially in other ways. I remember, for example, the word *dogmatic* was illustrated with a picture of a dog robot. Just as with the Pinky Lee show, these early experiences with words excited me because they showed how playful and creative one can be by combining two worlds—words and pictures— that are normally kept apart. There are many different ways for educators to bring together words and word meanings with pictures and images to help students increase their reading vocabulary. Here are a few activities that help students learn new words visually:

- Create "word art"—works of art that integrate painting, sculpture, or some other visual art form, with single words or phrases. Examples of this can be seen in early abstract art, such as in the paintings of Georges Braque and Marcel Duchamp, or more recently in the sculpture of Robert Indiana.

- Draw visual details on and around individual words to provide clues as to the meaning of the words. For example, a student might draw spokes in the loop of the *b* in the word *bike*, leaves dangling from the horizontal line in the letter *t* for the word *tree*, or lines radiating on all sides from the word *sun*. For examples of how this approach was used with a child labeled "learning disabled," see Cordoni (1981).

- Construct a visual image that connects an unfamiliar word and a familiar concrete word (similar in sound) that have some common feature. For example, in the word *carlin* (which means *old woman*), the student might visualize an old woman driving in a car (Baker, Simmons, and Kameenui, 1998).

- Define new vocabulary words by drawing pictures of each word's meaning on the back of a flash card that has that word on it. Alternatively, have students cut out pictures from magazines and paste them to the back of cards, or take photos of scenes that reveal each word's meaning and attach them to their vocabulary cards.

- Learn the spelling of new words by creating visually based stories. The cartoonist Chuck Close (who created the cartoon characters Wile E. Coyote and Road Runner) used this technique to get him through spelling class as a child. For example, to learn the spelling of the word *plankton*, he made up the following story: "**P**igs **L**eaping **A**round, **N**early **K**illing **T**en **O**ld **N**eighbors." He then visualized that scene whenever he needed to spell the word on a test (McGill, 1987).

- Find images on the Internet to define the meaning of unfamiliar words (use the image generator of any large search engine such as Google or AltaVista).

Picturing Sentences

As students begin to read and write sentences, they can transform the sentences into visual images or use images to create sentences in some of the following ways:

- Create sentence-long captions for photos, drawings, or pictures cut out of magazines.

- Draw single-scene cartoons with captions, or draw a cartoon strip with dialogue bubbles that contain sentence-length dialogue. The famed cartoonist Robert Ripley was allowed to hand in such word-filled cartoons in lieu of written reports in his high school in Santa Rosa, California, and later became one of the richest men in the world for his "Believe It or Not!" syndicated comic strip (Jackson, 1995).

- Create sentences that include visual emphasis of different kinds. For example, the sentence "The rocket ship blasted off into outer space" might use a dynamic font from a word processing program for the words "blasted off," or specific visual art effects such as debris, smoke, or fire drawn around these two words.

- Watch closed-captioned television shows or video programs that allow one to see the action, hear the words, and, at the same time, read the text of the dialogue at the bottom of the screen.

- Color code the parts of speech or other grammatical elements in a sentence (for example, all nouns colored blue, all verbs yellow, all adjectives green, all adverbs purple, etc.).

- Create computer-animated stories that contain words and sentences designed in highly colorful and visually dynamic ways.

Drawing on the Visual Imagery of Text

Many of the best writers in the world use stunning visual imagery in their text. Recently, for example, I was reading Marcel Proust's *Remembrance of Things Past*, a book considered by many to be one of the greatest novels ever written, and came upon this passage, which described the facial features of one of the characters in the novel, the Duke de Guermantes: "'What!'" he cried with fury, and indeed his face, convulsed and white, differed as much from his ordinary face as does the sea when on a morning of storm one finds instead of its customary smiling surface a thousand serpents writhing in spray and foam" (Proust, 1934, p. 1,111). This passage is just a particularly remarkable example of the kind of imagery that those who are about to embark upon the adventure of literacy are likely to encounter in their reading. Once students master reading single words and simple sentences and begin reading whole texts, the possibilities for visual-spatial learning become far more rich and complex.

Perhaps the simplest activity—and one that I believe would make a big difference in the reading comprehension rates of students, especially for those with good imaginations—would be to ask students anytime they have read a body of text to close their eyes for a minute or two and picture what they've just read. This practice gives students an immediate opportunity to visually process the material. Some students do this automatically as they read. Others may have great difficulty visualizing anything. However, for most students, setting aside short segments of time on a regular basis to visualize the material they've just read can provide an anchor to the text and ground it in a student's own perceptual experience.

To go one step further, students might be asked to *draw* their images of what they've just read, making quick one- to three-minute sketches or creating longer art projects (see Noden & Moss, 1995). Discussion of the reading material can then include not simply the spoken word, but reference to the students' internal visual imagery and to their external drawings (for example: "Mrs. Jones, I think that *Catcher in the Rye* reminds us to watch out for all the phoniness in this world. When I think of people who are phonies, I see faces with tight muscles and artificially smiling faces. And here's a picture I drew of the classic phony").

Another approach to employing visual imagery in reading involves the use of guided imagery to help students *into* the text. Before reading a text, let us say *Robinson Crusoe*, the teacher might take the students on an inner voyage in their imaginations where they are sailing on the sea and suddenly hit bad weather, and then end up shipwrecked on a strange coastline. This kind of guided imagery process allows the visual imagery of the students to create a sort of preparatory field (or what educator Madeline Hunter called "the anticipatory set") within which the Daniel Defoe classic can unfold as they begin to read the book. Students draw upon their own background of experiences as they engage in guided imagery activities in preparation for reading, and in doing so, are more likely to interact directly with the reading material as it is being studied (Harp, 1988).

Then there is the matter of using visual imagery—and in particular, drawing—in conjunction with *writing* activities. Unfortunately, drawing is usually relegated to inferior status in writing classes. The refrain usually goes "Write a 500-word story, and if you have time at the end, you can draw a picture." Alas, there is usually no time left for a picture! As Carroll (1991, p. 34) notes: "When we watch children in primary or elementary grades, we delight in all [their] drawing; we accept it as a way of meaning; we accept it as writing. 'Read what you have written,' we invite. So automatically . . . they read their circles with lines radiating out as 'a bright sunny day'; they read their row of stick figures as 'I love my family.' Yet somewhere up the ladder of academe, we educate out of students this powerful writing tool. We let middle- and high-school students know in subtle and sometimes not-so-subtle ways that drawing belongs to little kids."

Many students instinctively doodle as they write. Some keep personal journals that are records of both words and images (journals of this type were kept by illustrious picture-smart people such as Thomas Edison and Leonardo da Vinci). Educators need to incorporate more of students' drawings into their formal written work. In one New Hampshire project called "Image-Making Within the Writing Process," students create hand-painted textured paper that serves as the raw material for building colorful collage images. They weave story images using pictures and words in conjunction with these collage materials that they physically manipulate in sequencing the different episodes of their stories (Olshansky, 1994). Here are some other ways to incorporate pictures into the reading and writing process. Have students

- Use rebus texts that include a combination of words and rebuses (e.g., a picture of a bee for the word *be*). See the Peabody Rebus Reading Program, now out of print, which was based entirely on the use of rebuses (Woodcock, Clark, & Davies, 1968).

- Develop a written script for a movie and then videotape it. Or create a storyboard consisting of words and the sequence of images that make up the structure of the story, and then videotape it.

- Keep a regular "doodle diary" consisting of words and images as a way of taking notes during lectures in the classroom.

- Create formal illustrations to accompany science writing, geometric diagrams to accompany math writing, and illustrations to accompany fictional work.

- Study the illustrations of great literature, including the illustrations of Hablot Knight Browne (otherwise known as "Phiz") in

Charles Dickens's work, and the etchings accompanying William Blake's great poetic epics (Bindman, 2000).

- Illustrate particularly vivid visual metaphors used in literature (as in the example from Proust above).

Finding Books and Other Literacy Materials

The sort of books that appeal to visual-spatial individuals first and foremost have the feature of being heavily illustrated. Some "wordless" books consist of nothing but pictures, and are ideally suited to the highly picture-smart person who may be "word phobic" but who can approach a picture book with a sense of comfort and safety. There is very probably a continuum of books along the visual spectrum that extends from such wordless books through increasing levels of words per page, ending up with the completely pictureless books of literature and academe.

Of particular concern is the quality of the illustrations, again extending along a continuum from William Blake's masterpiece illustrations of his own work down to the poorly executed and artificial illustrations that often accompany classroom worksheets and workbooks. I remember one such poorly illustrated workbook from my elementary school days that showed the word *bacon*, whose meaning I could not make out because the picture displayed looked so grotesque that my visual sensibilities were offended and put up a mental roadblock to the word's semantic value. People being introduced to the world of literacy deserve to have their words accompanied by illustrations of merit. Examples of children's literature that link to the world of art include Michelle Dionetti's *Painting the Wind* (illustrated by Kevin Hawkes), Amy Littlesugar's *Marie in Fourth Position: The Story of Degas' "The Little Dancer"* (illustrated by Ian Schoenherr), and Aminah Brenda Lynn Robinson's fold-out book *A Street Called Home* (Gilles, 1998). But, even with this injunction for visual quality, there should still be some room left over for comic books—I learned to love several great works of literature initially by reading the Classic Comics versions. Increasingly, comics are becoming more sophisticated and serve as a basis for the illustration of complex topics like economics and calculus.

A further addition to the spatial richness of books comes with the inclusion of three-dimensional or "pop-up" books. One of my favorite 3-D books is Vicki Cobb's *Skyscraper Going Up*, which shows, in a series of pop-up pages, the various stages of building a skyscraper (with opportunities also to manipulate machinery involved in the construction process). Teachers and students can create their own pop-up books as art projects (see, for example, Jackson & Forrester, 1994). There are also books that come apart into puzzle pieces and can be reconstructed into castles, rocket ships, working clocks, or other three-dimensional objects. Finally, there are books that include some type of visual interaction, such as the Workman Publishers and Klutz Press books that come with painting sets, crayons, or other art materials attached and allow readers to draw or paint their own pictures in its pages.

Visual-Spatial Literacy Styles

As noted earlier, many individuals who excel in the arts, visual imagination, and other spatial abilities may have particular difficulty gaining entry into the world of literacy, and they may need special conditions to be met so that their experience of literacy can seem somehow more congruent with their artistic or pictorial proclivities. Too many of them feel roughly pushed out of their visual-spatial worlds onto a seemingly barren linguistic landscape. In addition to some of the activities listed above, here are some ways to bridge the gap between these two worlds:

- Allow students plenty of time to visualize, and even sketch, as they read.
- Give students access to the visual equivalent of a literary work as a supplementary resource. For example, if they are reading a novel, then provide the film treatment of the work if it exists. If there is a famously illustrated version of a particular literary work, then use that edition.
- Supply a variety of colored pencils for writing activities, and provide paper in a range of shapes and sizes.
- Give students time to illustrate their writing (for example, have them do the drawing *first*, and then the writing).

- Consider using colored backgrounds when showing text in an audiovisual format. When writing on the overhead, use a variety of colors (especially striking are transparencies and pens that show writing in *fluorescent* colors).

- Use color to highlight phrases, special words, word patterns, and other reading components. Allow the students to use colored backgrounds and letters when writing and reading text on a computer (Viau, 1998). Let them experiment with colored gels (colored transparent sheets) placed over book texts (see Irlen, 1991).

For Further Study

- Ask students to describe what goes on visually in their heads as they read specific text. Note individual differences. Try this experiment with different types of text that vary in their visual richness from highly descriptive literature to abstract textbook material.

- Develop a library of literacy materials that integrate visual images in different ways into the text (for example, wordless books, pop-up books, and books one can draw in). Seek maximum visual variety in the types of books and other literacy materials you select.

- Set up a center in your classroom or school that integrates writing with art (you might call it the William Blake Center in honor of one of the world's greatest artist-poets), where students can create word sculptures, comic books, illustrated storybooks, geometric poetry, and other word-image projects.

- Create a phonics program that links phonemes to specific visual images, shapes, or colors.

- Generate a list of 10 to 20 difficult vocabulary words for your students, and then use a variety of visual strategies to help students learn them (for example, creating visual associations or drawing pictures of each word).

- Provide verbal material in the classroom that is visually capti-
  vating (for example, colorful handouts, bulletin boards that
  include words that are visually dynamic, and tests that use interesting fonts and colors).

4

Grooving with the Rhythms of Language

Notice how, this sentence is particularly; difficult to, read because, I; have put in, punctuation, marks that, disturb the, basic, flow of what I am, trying to, say. Whereas, when I place the punctuation marks appropriately, my ability to communicate effectively with you becomes much smoother. This little experiment provides a small indication of the huge importance that rhythm, meter, and music have in language and literacy. Although we may be aware of it only when we hear someone sing or recite poetry, or when we hear violations of the natural rhythm of language as noted above, it's still true that all the words that come out of our mouths (as well as the lines that emerge from our pens and word processors) ride upon a stream of music. To help individuals achieve literacy, it seems critically important that we acknowledge this important connection between words and music and use it as fully as we can to help our students read and write more effectively

Some theorists have suggested that language itself emerged out of musical expression. Charles Darwin proposed that humans' predecessors "courted each other by the aid of vocal tones" (Darwin, 1910, p. 217).

Vaneechouette & Skoyles (1998) theorize that communication through singing in birds, apes, and humans facilitated mating, social bonding, and other behaviors important to reproduction, and that such traits for vocal/musical communicative ability were retained by natural selection in the course of evolution. We can also observe the fundamental importance of music as a means of communication in the development of cultures historically. Before the advent of literacy, much verbal information was communicated from generation to generation through chants, rhythms, and other musical and prosodic forms. Some of the greatest and earliest literary works, including *The Iliad* and the *The Odyssey* by Homer, and the Hebrew Bible, were originally orally transmitted through rhythmic methods of recitation. The Greeks placed a great deal of importance upon metered verse in both oral and written communication, developing a whole catalogue of rhythmic forms to convey different types of moods and content. Such rhythmic underpinnings were crucial to the sense of the spoken or written passages. During antiquity and into the Middle Ages, reading was rarely silent in the way we understand it today, but rather a kind of incantation, according to McLuan (1965, p. 84).

Old English was remarkable for its alliterative qualities. Anglo-Saxon verse, for example, consisted of two parts bound together by alliteration (for example, in *Beowulf*: Gréndel góngan, Gódes yrre bæ'r: "Grendel walking, he bore God's anger"). As modern English began to evolve, William Shakespeare demonstrated in his 37 plays how much music and rhythm still remained in the language. For example, Shakespeare varies the rhythms in his plays according to social class (the aristocracy speaks in iambic pentameter, while the lower classes speak in prose or choppier meters). In his play *A Midsummer Night's Dream*, he creates rhythmic disturbances in his verse whenever the moon is mentioned, because the moon is known to create lunatics and therefore must do something similar to the flow of words. For example, notice how the iambic pentameter (ta-TA/ta-TA/ta-Ta/ta-TA/ta-Ta) is interrupted by the words "cold moon" in this passage from Act 2, Scene 1: "That very time I saw (but thou couldst not)/Flying between the cold moon and the earth."

In contemporary times, much of the rhythmic content of the English language has been lost in the homogenization of speech rhythms (perhaps aided and abetted by the media, which excels in providing a constant drone to our assaulted ears). However, we still hear the rhythms of music stir words to life in our great orators (remember Martin Luther King Jr.'s historic "I Have a Dream" speech), and in our best writers and poets. Children's literature pioneer Dr. Seuss recalled that it was listening to the clackety-clackety-clack of the railroad moving along the tracks during a trip that inspired the rhythms for many of his wonderful children's books (you can almost hear that train echo in the rhythms of: "And to think that I saw it on Mulberry street"). British poet Stephen Spender wrote of how a language of music and rhythms emerged during his creative reveries: "Sometimes, when I lie in a state of half-waking half-sleeping, I am conscious of a stream of words which seem to pass through my mind, without their having a meaning, but they have a sound, a sound of passion, or a sound recalling poetry that I know. Again sometimes when I am writing, the music of the words I am trying to shape takes me far beyond the words, I am aware of a rhythm, a dance, a fury, which is as yet empty of words" (Ghiselin, 1960, p. 124).

This sensitivity to the music of words begins very early in life, perhaps even before birth. Studies show that newborns can discriminate the rhythm of multisyllabic stressed words, suggesting that they're already sensitized to word rhythms from the mother's voice in utero (Sansavini, Bertoncini, & Giovanelli, 1997). Mothers and other caregivers have a natural tendency to speak to infants in rhythmic, intonated, and rhymed cadences ("Such a *sweetie* little baby). And infants and young children play with the rhythms of language as they begin to babble and speak. In their first literacy experiences, parents generally don't read to a child in a monotone voice from a car repair manual or the Encyclopaedia Britannica, but rather from nursery rhymes, rhythmic stories, songbooks, and other musical-verbal forms. As young children develop in their speaking ability, they begin to create their own interesting words and phrases that reflect this musical background as well as their own emerging mental structures.

Werner (1973) writes about two young English children who contrived their own language. The word *bal* meant *place*. As they varied the intonation of the vowel, the size of the place changed. The longer they stretched out the vowel, the larger the place indicated, so that tonal variations in the same word could mean *village*, *town*, or *city*. Their word for *going* was *dudu* and the quicker it was said, the faster was the going, so that "Du-u-du-u" meant to go slowly. Werner also writes about children who developed their own onomatopoetic words, such as the three-and-a-half-year old who said: "Mother, we're going over *nubbles*" (a sidewalk made of small uniformly cut stones half-buried in the ground) and "Mother, you *rhost* so!" (*rhost* referring to the scraping sound made by shoes on gravel). As children enter school, these musical-verbal connections can help them in their acquisition of literacy. One study suggested that sensitivity to rhyme and alliteration leads to awareness of phonemes and the ability to read (Bryant, MacLean, Bradley, & Crossland, 1990). Another study indicated that those individuals best able to detect modulations, or shifts in pitch, of low-frequency sounds, prove best at reading words (Talcott et al., 2000). Some of the most recent research in the study of individuals labeled as dyslexic indicates their greatest difficulties are phonological-musical, particularly in reading rhymed nonsense words (Shaywitz et al., 1998).

Cellular circuits that recognize language and music are found on both sides of the brain, in the auditory cortex of each hemisphere (though the left auditory cortex also contains regions exclusively dedicated to language while the right cortex has areas set aside just for music). The features that music and words share in the brain include meter, duration, contour, and timbral similarity, whereas syntax and semantics for language, and musical pitch relations for music are generally not shared systems (Lerdahl, 2001). However, one study indicated that altering the intonation in verbal speech or the punctuation in reading passages also influenced the subjects' comprehension of sentence structure and the semantic encoding of individual words, a finding that appears to support the results of our little experiment that began this chapter (Cohen, Douaire, & Elsabbagh, 2001). In studies of individuals with specific language difficulties, including stuttering and aphasia, music and rhythm have often been seen as important factors in reducing symptoms, thus allowing individuals to speak or comprehend language more fluently (see for example, Kimelman, 1999). These studies suggest that words and music do have important connections in the brain that can facilitate the processing of language and literacy.

Putting Musical Pizzazz into Letters and Sounds

Because research suggests that many individuals who struggle with reading have difficulty discriminating between phonemes in initially attempting to read (Shaywitz et al., 1998), then phonemic approaches that help accentuate the sounds of these phonemes may go a long way in helping many of these people acquire literacy. One group of researchers has developed a computer learning system that artificially slows down the pronunciation of these phonemes so that students can better hear the differences between them (Greenwald, 1999). Teachers can provide less expensive and more interpersonally interactive ways of accomplishing the same thing by engaging students in activities that bring out the musical qualities of phonemes to provide a means of distinguishing between them (see Yopp & Yopp, 1997). Here is an example of a song that helps students discriminate between vowel sounds. Its initial version goes like this:

> (G C D E/ E   FE   D C E D)
> I want to eat/Eight apples and bananas
> (G B C D/ D   E D   C B D C)
> I want to eat/Eight apples and bananas

Subsequent versions substitute a specific vowel sound (e.g. "ee" or "oo") for most of the vowels in the song. For example:

> Ee ween tee eet/Eet Eeples and beeneenees
> Ee ween tee eet/Eet Eeples and beeneenees

Or alternatively,

> Oo woon too oot/Oot ooples and boonoonoos
> Oo woon too oot/Oot ooples and boonoonoos

Another approach is to take songs that are popular with the students, print out the song lyrics, identify particular phonemes that you'd like to help students distinguish (such as "b," "p," and "d") and then highlight those particular phonemes in color on the lyric sheet. Then, when singing the song, emphasize those particular phonemes by (for example) spitting out on the "p," "b," and "d" sounds (make sure to do this outdoors!). The supplementary use of visual cards to show placement of the mouth (as in the Lindamood phoneme sequencing program; see McGuinness, 1985) can help cue students as to how their mouths should be formed for each phoneme. Here are some other ideas:

- Use songs about phonemes that can help students become sensitive to the differences (for example, for vowel substitutions, the song, "Wiloughby Wallaby Woo" by the songwriter Raffi).

- Employ tongue twisters and alliterative verses that provide reinforcement of specific phonemic sounds.

- Have students create their own musical compositions using only phonemes in rhythmic patterns (e.g., "buh buh buh/puh puh puh/duh duh duh duh").

Finally, to help students learn the alphabet, there are a wide range of songs, songbooks, and activities (see, for example, Raschke, Alper, & Eggers, 1999).

Enjoying the Delicious Music of Words

One of the most wonderful things about words is the way they sound. Cur-mudg-e-on. Hob-nob. Buzz. Rum-pus. Stomp. Fan-ta-size. Sometimes, as teachers, we get so focused on teaching students the *meanings* and *spellings* of words that we don't take time to help students sit back and just savor the delicious flavors of the sounds of words. The closest we get is when we help students syllabify words—then we begin to approach words with a sense of rhythm. But often the focus is on counting the number of syllables (a logical-mathematical approach) rather than on realizing the flow of the word through our lips. As students begin to appreciate the tremendous diversity of sounds that fill our language, they are more likely to show interest in their inner workings (semantics, syntax), much as a person who begins to appreciate the music of Beethoven seeks to find out more about his life and times. Here are a number of ways that teachers can help sensitize students to the musicality of English words:

- Have students create a song or rap from this week's vocabulary list.

- Introduce students to a wide range of particularly onomatopoetic words. Let them find their own examples. Finally, let them create poetry by using these words and by making up their own onomatopoetic words.

- Let students come up with their Favorite-Sounding Word of the Week.

- When reading a text, take time out to appreciate the sounds of particularly interesting words. Look for authors and texts that emphasize the sounds of words. My own particular favorite is James Joyce's novel *Finnegans Wake*. Joyce creates many of his own words in this book based in part upon their delicious sound value (for example, to represent the sound of thunder, and man's fall from the Garden of Eden) he wrote: "babadadalgharaght-akamminarronnkonnbronntonnerronntuonnthunntrovar-rhounawnskawntoohoohoordenenthurnuk!" (Joyce, 1969, p. 3).

- When teaching syllabification, let students use percussion instruments to tap out the syllables.

In addition to these suggestions, music can assist teachers more directly with word meaning and spelling in some of the following ways (see Prichard & Taylor, 1980):

- Have students sit back with their eyes closed and listen to some slow and regular piece of music (for example, any classical piece in 4/4 time, such as the Largo from Handel's opera *Xerxes*, or Pachelbel's Canon in D). Then, repeat the week's vocabulary words and their meanings slowly in time to the music.

- Teach spelling words to the sound of music. For example, any seven-letter word (or multiple of seven letters) can be sung to the tune of "Twinkle Twinkle Little Star" (for example, "S-n-i-p-p-e-t, s-n-i-p-p-e-t . . ."). For six-letter words, use "Happy Birthday to You," for five-letter words use "Row, Row, Row Your Boat," for four-letter words, "The Happy Wanderer," for three-letter words, "Three Blind Mice."

- Spell words rhythmically to a metronome, to background music, or to percussion instrument sounds created by the class.

Making Sentences Move to Music

Any sentence can become the lyrics of a piece of music or a rhythmic chant, including this one. Try it! Knowing this simple fact can turn a boring grammar lesson or other literacy lesson using single sentences into a musical or rhythmic festival! Here are some ways to make music a part of grammar lessons:

- Chant individual sentences with the student or class, using a drum or other percussion instrument to bang out the rhythms.

- Sing popular songs, but change the syntax to reflect the objectives of the grammar lesson (for example, to learn verb tenses, sing "Michael Rowed the Boat Ashore," "Michael Will Row the Boat Ashore," "Michael Has Rowed the Boat Ashore," "Michael Would Have Rowed the Boat Ashore," and so on).

- Teach adjectives using rhythmic chanting based upon an old British social game called "The Minister's Cat" (an example of this game being played is shown in the movie *Scrooge* with Albert Finney). Participants sit in a circle and begin clapping their hands in a regular beat (not too fast at first). Then the person to start says in time to the beat: "The Min-is-ter's Cat is a lov-a-ble beast." Without missing the beat, the next person must continue this rhythm with a different adjective: "The Min-is-ter's Cat is a cap-a-ble beast" and so on down the line. Anyone who fails to keep up the beat drops out, with the game resuming until only one person is left. This basic structure can be made simpler (with one- or two syllable adjectives) or harder as needed to suit the particular group of students.

- As a class, read sentences out loud (the students should have written copies of the sentences in front of them). As each punctuation mark is reached, students should make a specific sound (e.g., commas might be "pops," and periods might be "Bronx cheers") to represent that mark (the musical comedian Victor Borge used this method in his comedy routines).

One particular movement that has accomplished a great deal to bring together rhythm, music, and language is the Orff-Schulwerk approach. A basic tenet of the Orff-Schulwerk approach (*schulwerk* is German for schoolwork) is that students should begin with their own speech and song heritage—rhymes and proverbs, children's chants and games, and song. Much is done with musical patterns linked with verbal phrases, often using percussion instruments that have been specifically designed for this work (see Nash, 1974; Shamrock, 1986).

Making the Text Come Alive with the Sound of Music

When I taught special education classes in California in the 1980s, I often began my classes with music and words. Students would come into class and see the lyrics to a song on their desk. Usually it was a song that was based upon their own kid culture. I knew, for example, that my students loved the television show "The Dukes of Hazzard," so one day the lyrics for the theme song of that program, written by Waylon Jennings, were waiting there for them to read and sing. These song lyrics became text, with as much validity as the text in their basal readers, in their library books, and in their special education materials. In fact, it had more validity because it had more *vitality*. I was disappointed at the time to see that only one formal reading program was based upon song lyrics. The program was limited to Donny and Marie Osmond songs.

Today, a search of the educational databases indicates *no* reading programs based primarily on music and song lyrics. Why is this so? Perhaps they would be too expensive to produce (with money required to reprint song lyrics and recorded music). However, I also think that part of the reason is that there is the sense in education that music is a frill and that, aside from small doses of it in cute little songs and rhymes, formal reading programs are much too serious to be bothered by this kind of creative nonsense. And yet, for the highly musical individual who struggles with reading using traditional methods, such a program might well be the magic key that gives them access to the world of literacy. Because there isn't a formal reading program based solely on music, the next best thing is for teachers to create their own informal methods for exploring text using music as a primary learning tool (for excellent resources see, for example, Rivard & Bieske, 1993; Wallace, 1992; McCracken & McCracken, 1998; Paul, 2000; Fisher, McDonald, & Strickland, 2001; Fisher & McDonald, 2001).

A good starting place is to pay attention to the music that is "playing" in a text. It's amazing how often music, or musical sounds, or references to music, take place in literature and nonfiction works. Look for musical metaphors, such as when Rosalind says in Act 4, Scene 3 of Shakespeare's *As You Like It*: "What, to make thee an instrument and play false strains upon thee! not to be endured!" Students can play around with such a metaphor—for example, a person might hold a violin while someone else comes up to them with a bow and plays dissonant sounds as they speak Rosalind's line. Also, look for music being played in the background of a text, and then find some recorded music that reproduces these sounds. I remember teaching S. E. Hinton's novel *That Was Then, This Is Now* to a group of high school students, and there was a scene where some popular music was being played. I asked the students if they had any recorded music we could use to recreate this scene, and at least 10 students immediately took out cassette tapes and CDs from their bags and purses! If specific pieces are played in the background of a text, or the characters refer to a specific musical work, it can accentuate the experience of reading to bring in that piece to supplement the text. There is, for example, a CD recording of well-known Irish songs that appear in various pieces of James Joyce's writing (*Joyce's Parlour Music: 13 Songs of the Time* available through Maginni Enterprises, 24 Vernon Street, Dublin 8, Ireland).

Also, look for environmental sounds in texts, such as rain falling, the wind blowing against the trees, or the sound of an avalanche. These sounds can be recreated using sound effects made by the students, or by using sound effects tapes borrowed from a public library or imported from the Internet. In fact, a class might even create a sound effects library of materials to use in putting on plays or in providing sound effects during the reading of other texts. Sound effects can also be a useful way to help students remember the sequence of key events or passages in a story. In my work with teachers, I often ask them to help me re-create a five-part story using background sound effects:

> Part 1. It was a dark and stormy night. ("shhh. . . krrr. . .")
> Part 2. There was a knock on the door. ("knock, knock, knock")
> Part 3. A shot rang out. ("Bang!")
> Part 4. A cry was heard. ("Yeek!")
> Part 5. It was the opera lady. (Laaa!")

We practice each part with the audience providing the sound effects appropriate to each scene. Then, after going through the five parts verbally, I signal for the group to tell me the story nonverbally through the sound effects ("shhh. . . krrr. . . knock, knock, knock. . . Bang! . . . Yeek! . . . Laaa!") Teachers can do the same thing for more complex stories, novels, or other narratives to help students remember the flow of the plot or the development of a character. One might, for example, tell the story of a specific character's rise and fall using percussion instruments. Many famous symphonic works were written with the idea of creating a story. Beethoven's *Pastoral Symphony* loosely tells the musical story of a group of peasants out for a picnic in nature until a storm interrupts their festivities. Hector Berlioz tells Shakespeare's most famous love story in his symphonic poem *Romeo and Juliet* (the clashing of instruments parallels the feud between the Capulets and the Montagues). Here are a few other strategies that can help put the musical pizzaz back in reading and writing:

- Have students keep Musical Response Journals where they write about their experiences listening to different musical pieces (Kolb, 1996).

- Select text that is especially rhythmic and read it out loud. Great examples include poems and stories by Edgar Allan Poe, Lewis Carroll, Samuel Taylor Coleridge, Ogden Nash, and Dr. Seuss.

- As a text is being read out loud, have students listen to the rhythms and comment on their experiences (for example, differentiating between texts that have smooth versus choppy rhythms).

- Let students write song lyrics as part of their regular writing activities.

- Take text that is especially boring (such as textbook material), and as a group rhythmically chant it out loud as if it were a musical work being performed in a symphony hall.

- Get software programs (such as karaoke software) that allow students to sing a song while they read the lyrics on screen.

- Use dialogue in text as an opportunity to play around creatively with rhythms, dialects, and intonations.

Books and Other Literacy Materials for the Musical Learner

Stock your literacy or reading program library with books and other literacy materials that reflect musical themes in some way—works that would be likely to draw in a word-phobic person who has lively musical interests. Songbooks top the list, ideally with recordings available to support them. For younger children, song picture books such as *Eat Your Peas, Louise!* by Pegeen Snow, provide rhyme, rhythm, and repetition of vocabulary and story structure to reinforce literacy skills (Barclay & Walwer, 1992). There are also books that include embedded computerized keyboards along with a color-coded notation system and lyrics to the music—so that readers can read and play the music all within the covers of one book. Another group of books come with musical instruments attached in a bag, such as John Gindick's *Country & Blues Harmonica for the Musically Hopeless* (Klutz Press). There are also books that include musical themes in their content, such as Bernardine Connelly's *Follow the Drinking Gourd: A Story of the Underground Railroad*, which is based on the traditional folk song "Follow the Drinking Gourd." Finally, any musical literacy library should include plenty of poetry (including recordings of the poets reading their work out loud), as well as other books and programs that include songs, rhymes, rhythms, raps, alliteration, and other ways of making the words come alive with the sound of music

Musical Literacy Styles

The writer Hart Crane used to write on his typewriter while playing phonograph records of Cuban rumbas, torch songs, and classical works such as Maurice Ravel's *Bolero* (Ghiselin, 1960). His writing habits suggest one way that educators might treat highly musical individuals when they are engaged in literacy activities: allow them to listen to music when they read and write, and let them select the music whenever possible. Research suggests that music can help focus certain individuals, such as those identified as having attention deficit hyperactivity disorder (see Cripe, 1986). Provide students with the freedom to sing, hum, or talk out loud as they read or write if they need to. Some highly musical readers and writers may want to tap their fingers, move their feet rhythmically, let their body rock, or in other ways groove to the words they are reading or writing. Again, provide an environment that is conducive to this activity. The silent classroom, while considered an exemplary model to many school administrators, may not provide the proper atmosphere within which certain musical individuals can adequately develop their literacy skills. Consider providing a rocking chair, hammock, or other rhythmic place to relax in while engaged in reading. Ideally, a literacy program should, at least part of the time, be rockin' the aisles with the music of words!

For Further Study

- Put on a poetry slam or songwriting contest where students can write and perform their work before a supportive audience (see Glazner, 2000).

- Develop a music program based upon favorite songs of the students in the classroom. Select vocabulary words from the lyrics, create phonics lessons based upon selected words, and help students plot the sequence of the story (if there is one) for each song. Let students write alternative lyrics to the songs, and develop other reading and writing skills based on this material.

- Create a song or chant based upon the 44 phonemes of the English language (or some judicious selection of phonemes based upon the phonological needs of individual students) and teach it to your class.

- Surprise your students one day by singing or chanting a text that you are reading to them. Have students share their reactions, and use the discussion as an opportunity to talk about the music of words.

- Develop a list of "programme music" (instrumental works such as Berlioz's *Symphonie Fantastique* or Beethoven's *Pastoral Symphony* that tell a story) to play to your class. Play Prokofiev's *Peter and the Wolf* along with the verbal commentary by Leonard Bernstein (*Bernstein Favorites Children's Classics,* Sony). Then invite your students to create their own musical stories using simple musical instruments.

5

Calculating the Logic of Words

The British playwright George Bernard Shaw, in an attempt to reveal the inconsistencies of English spelling and to advance his own phonetic reforms of the language, once pointed out that under the "rules" of English spelling, it would be perfectly sensible to spell the word *fish* as *ghoti*. His reasoning went something like this: if you took the "gh" from *cough*, the "o" in *women*, and the "ti" in *nation*, then "gh-o-ti" would have the same sound equivalence as "f-i-sh." His point is well taken. Whereas other languages such as Italian and the Japanese *kana* script have much simpler and direct correspondences of sound to symbol, English, it seems, is all over the place. There are more than 1,100 ways that letters in English can be used to symbolize the 44 sounds in the spoken language. This diversity gives rise to sentences that would baffle just about anyone trying to learn the code. Some examples: "The bandage was wound around the wound." "The farm was used to produce produce." "The soldier decided to desert his dessert in the desert." One brain scan study indicated that countries with complex writing systems (including the United States and the United Kingdom) have the highest prevalence of people showing symptoms of dyslexia (Venis, 2001). So, on the surface, at least, English is certainly not a logical code.

The Logic of Language

Under the surface, however, it's a very different picture. Largely because of the brilliant work of MIT professor Noam Chomsky beginning in the 1950s, most linguists now believe that there are universal logical rules, computations, and transformations that underlie virtually every language in the world, and that children instinctively reveal their understanding of this logic as they begin to put words together in speech. Listen to a 3-year-old speak after she's spied a robin perched in a tree. She'll say something like "Birdie on tree." You won't hear her say "Tree birdie on" or "On birdie tree" or even "Tree on birdie." How is it that she knows the correct order in which to put these three words? You might say that it's because she's heard someone say the phrase "birdie on tree." And yet, in studies where preschoolers are told: "Here is a wug. Now there are two of them. There are two ____ ," the kids unflinchingly respond, "Two wugs." They've never heard anyone say that word before, and yet somehow they know the underlying rule about adding an *s*. In one study, an experimenter controlled a doll of Jabba the Hut from the movie *Star Wars*, while children were coaxed to ask Jabba questions concerning different scenarios. One prompt was quite complex: "Ask Jabba if the boy who is unhappy is watching Mickey Mouse;" The children easily responded: "Is the boy who is unhappy watching Mickey Mouse?" How did they know to take the second "is" in the prompt and make it the first word in the question? They could have just as easily taken the first "is" and made it: "Is the boy who unhappy is watching Mickey Mouse?" (Pinker, 1994). Yet, that wouldn't have made sense. Chomsky says that children come into the world biologically equipped with the logical apparatus needed to quickly and easily unravel and solve such linguistic puzzles (Chomsky, 1994-5).

Scientists still do not know the exact neurological locus for these underlying abilities. Traditionally it had been thought that Broca's area in the lower frontal lobe of the left hemisphere was the center of syntax in the brain, based upon clinical studies of aphasics who had lesions in that area of the brain, and whose syntactic expression literally fell apart as a result of the damage (Gardner, 1974). While Broca's area and adjacent regions are still seen as crucial in syntactic processing, especially for the kinds of transformations in grammar that Chomsky wrote about (see, for example, Embick, Marantz, Miyashita, O'Neal, & Sakai, 2000; Indefrey et al., 2001), other studies indicate that syntactic production also extends to other language centers in the left hemisphere, including Wernicke's area and the angular gyrus (Grodzinsky, 2000; Sakai, Hashimoto, & Homae, 2001).

The Reader as Scientist

As children move into the world of print they carry their sophisticated knowledge of the underlying structures of grammar with them. Psycholinguist Frank Smith has compared children learning to read with scientists creating and testing hypotheses (Smith, 1996). As a child reads and encounters new words, she sets up little experiments. She sees a word she doesn't know—*clothes*, for example, in the sentence "The girl got out of the tub and put on her clothes." If she's a good phonetic decoder she might read "clo-th-ess" and be puzzled. "Hmm . . . that's not a word that I've ever heard . . . maybe it's something close to that . . . clo-thess . . . colthess . . . clot . . . clots . . . The girl put on her clots. No that doesn't make sense . . . let's look at the sentence. Hmmmm. The girl is doing something . . . putting something on . . . putting on her clogs? Wait. I think she's getting dressed . . . she's putting on her . . . oh yes! She's putting on her *clothes*!" Just as the scientist gathers data, and may at first look at it with puzzlement, wondering how to make sense of it in the larger scope of things until eventually relating it in a consistent way to other data that he has acquired, so too the child is involved in accumulating data from a text, and trying to make it all coalesce into some kind of overall meaning.

In order to do this, she has to call upon all sorts of skills— phonological ("clo-th-ess"), syntactical ("the girl is putting on something"), and semantic ("clots? clogs? clothes!")—in order to solve her problem. Wernicke's area and other language areas in the left hemisphere of her cerebral cortex are part of her semantic base in coming up with the appropriate meaningful word. In addition, recent research indicates that areas of the right hemisphere are also useful in the initial processes of determining the meaning of ambiguous words (especially concrete nouns) and text (Beeman & Bowden, 2000; Shibahara & Lucero-Wagoner, 2001; Chiarello, Liu, & Faust, 2001; Kircher, Brammer, Tous Andreu, Williams, & McGuire, 2001; Coney, 2002). Right hemispheric areas homologous to those in the left hemisphere may be involved in the processing of loose word associations ("clots? clogs?") and also in visualizing contexts or scenarios in which these words may or may not fit (the thought "I think she's getting dressed" may have been accompanied, for example, by a visual image of someone getting into her clothes). Because most brain research has been conducted only on single words and sentences, there has been a tendency to neglect the role of the right hemisphere in reading situations that involve the continuous reading of paragraphs where the process of problem solving requires complex interactions between hemispheres (and these situations make up just about all of the real reading contexts that literate people engage in).

Discovering the Logic (and Illogic) of Letters and Sounds

Most phonics programs in schools and literacy programs today present sound-symbol correspondences in a systematic manner. Their primary objective is to highlight what is most predictable about the sound-symbol relationships in the English language, and to teach these orderly patterns to students in a logical way. Thank goodness there is much in the language that is, in fact, predictable! We know, for example, that the letter *b* in the word *bat* will pretty much remain consistent no matter which other set of letters we put it in front of (*baby*, *boy*, *balloon*, *belch*, and so on). For the letter *p*, in the word *pat*, however, it's a slightly more complicated matter. To this letter, we have to apply a rule, that if the *p* is followed by an *h*, it will have a different sound ("ph" as in *phonics*). With vowels, the matter becomes even murkier. We still do have quite a number of logical patterns that we can teach students. For example, the short "e" sound in *pet* will be replicated in the words *set*, *let*, and *get*, and the short "o" sound in *pot*, *rot*, and *lot*. So there's something akin to a scientific law going on here. However, then we reach the "silent *e*" and attempt to formulate a rule: "when a word has a silent *e* at the end, the previous vowel has a long

71

sound," as in the words *pave, gave, save,* and *wave.* This pattern sounds nice and predictable, but then the student discovers the words *have, done, some,* and *were.* They don't fit the pattern. They're exceptions to the rule. One of the most famous sounding-out rules of all: "When two vowels go walking, the first one does the talking" has an exception to the rule ("does") right in its own definition.

Most standard reading programs attempt to teach phonetic patterns, rules, and their long lists of exceptions in a teacher-directed way. Another approach that might be used, especially with students who have particularly logical proclivities, would be to allow the students to discover many of these patterns and rules for themselves. We encourage students in critical thinking programs and math classes to work with logical games involving numbers such as "What's My Rule?" (for example, a list of numbers is presented—3, 6, 9, 12, 15—and the student must give a rule, such as "you add three to a number and get the next number"). Why not do the same thing with letters, sounds, and words? For example, in a game called "What's My Phonetic Rule?" students might be provided with a list of three words—*pot, lot, got*—and then asked what rule or pattern links them (they rhyme, they all have an *o* in the middle, they all have the same vowel sound, and so on). Then, the teacher can ask students if they can predict what *r-o-t* might sound like based on their rules. For more complex examples, students can be challenged to find the exceptions to the rule. This approach treats phonics as an adventure in problem solving rather than simple rote memorization.

Dissecting Words in the Laboratory

As students advance beyond letter-sound correspondences to actual word attack skills, their ability to decode can be strengthened by continuing to use logical strategies in unraveling words and their meanings. Understanding structural units or morphemes in words, including prefixes (*un-, dis-, non-, in-*) and suffixes (*-ing, -ly, -s*), can help students engage in a logical dissection or analysis of a word to reveal its constituent parts. So, when students see the word *misunderstanding,* they will have tools to break it into simpler units (*mis+under+stand+ing*), just as a math student might break apart a complex math problem such as $4(2+4)-7+(68) = x$ into a simpler form: $(4 \times 6) - (7+68) = x$. Deshler,

Ellis, and Lenz (1996) suggest students use an overall cognitive strategy when attempting to identify an unfamiliar word, including the use of a 3's rule (if the first letter in the stem begins with a consonant, underline three letters) and a 2's rule (if the first letter in the stem begins with a vowel, underline two letters). So, for the word *jurisprudence* the student would underline *jur* and *is* to assist with his attack on the word. Knowledge of root words can also provide a tremendous boost to dissecting an unfamiliar word and getting at its underlying meaning (for example, knowing that *juris* is related to *jury* and *jurists* and that *prudence* means *cautious* or *careful* can help a person make an educated guess as to the meaning of *jurisprudence*).

Examining the context of the word in the text is also an important part of the logical problem-solving process in reading. Looking at the words a student does know in a passage and making predictions and inferences about what the unfamiliar word might be based on those words and other cues (including pictures) also reveals a logical approach to word attack (see Goodman & Marek, 1996). For example, if students read: "The men carried large amphoras filled with olive oil onto the loading ramp of the large ship," then they might reason that the word *amphora* has to be some kind of container (which it is). Even in understanding some of the more irrational aspects of the English language, such as why we add *-tion* and *-ick* endings to some words, an explanation based upon history may help satisfy the highly logical student (The Vikings introduced the "-ick" spelling into the language in the 9th century, and the French brought in the "-tion" spelling with the Norman Conquest of 1066). This is also true of word meanings. By looking up a word in a comprehensive etymological dictionary such as the *Oxford English Dictionary*, a student can learn the origins of a word in other languages and how the meaning and spelling of a word have changed over hundreds of years. By understanding that words have a historical context, their rule-breaking character is at the very least given a causal explanation.

Making Sense of Sentences

As students begin to put words together into sentences that they read or write, new kinds of logical structures come into play. There are, for example, the syntactical structures embedded into sentences of the kind that Chomsky and his colleagues have written about (Chomsky, 1957; Pinker, 1994). I remember diagramming sentences based upon Chomsky's paradigm in high school English classes in the late 1960s. They called it "transformational grammar," or "T-grammar," and it was probably the literary equivalent of "the new math" movement in the 1960s; in both cases, research by intellectuals had inspired a wave of practical applications across American classrooms. Today, both "the new math" and "T-grammar" are practically nonexistent in the education research literature, and in most classrooms. However, I think there is a place for such analytic approaches, especially for students who have logical-mathematical proclivities. By diagramming the structural components of a sentence, students have an opportunity to see the sentence's underlying logical units, and this can help them to use these units to create other linguistic combinations. One of the most fascinating findings of Chomsky's work was that a finite set of linguistic structures can generate an infinite number of possible sentences. Knowing this, students can be empowered to explore the infinite powers of expression inherent in language through an analysis of its component parts. So, for example, one can read this sentence:

A tiny ferocious white cat peered out the window.

and diagram it into its appropriate modules (Figure 5.1).

Then, through an understanding of the underlying logical structures it becomes possible to engage in an infinite number of substitutions: *A large stupid brown bear crawled out the porthole. Out [of] the aperture stumbled a humongous rabid chartreuse aardvark.* Students just starting out can begin with simpler syntactic formations such as Subject/Verb/Object, and create a wide range of substitutions, perhaps making one substitution per transformation: The man ate the banana. The *girl* ate the banana. The girl ate the *grapes*. The girl *grabbed* the grapes. The *ape* grabbed the grapes. The ape grabbed the *apple*. And so on.

Another logical way of approaching sentences involves focusing on the *meaning* of sentences. This, in fact, has been one of the primary avenues of exploration in the field of philosophy for the past 100 years or so, as analytic philosophers have attempted to articulate "truth" and

Figure 5.1

Diagram of a Sentence

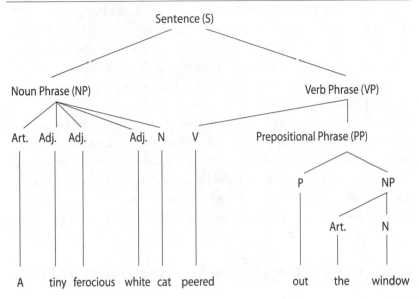

do away with 2,500 years of metaphysical speculations in philosophy by attempting to create logical or empirically verifiable sentences (see, for example, Ayer, 1952). "The man is tall," for example, is something that can be verified (you can measure the man and if he's six feet, seven inches high, bingo!). "The man is a human being" is something that doesn't need to be verified, on the other hand, because we already know that *every man is a human being*, so it's simply logical that this sentence is true (this is what analytic philosophers call a "tautology"). But if we say something like "The tarantula had a dream that it ate a turkey sandwich at Carnegie Hall," what do we do with that? We can't empirically verify it, because spiders can't talk to us. And it doesn't make a lot of sense in other ways—as far as we know, spiders don't eat turkey sandwiches, nor do they dream.

In the classroom, students who have logical proclivities may be interested in thinking about and creating both logical and illogical sentences. For example, you might show students several sentences, and ask them to put them in one of two categories, True or False, and then discuss their reasons for doing so. Or students might be invited to write sentences that they believe are absolutely 100 percent true, and then defend their reasons against all challenges ("You say: 'It was a great day yesterday.' How do you know that? It wasn't great for me! What does 'great' mean anyway?"). Or students can play around with the logic of words precisely by creating nonsensical sentences (or non-sentences!), like "The elbow kicked the soccer ball into the thimble," which might then be discussed in terms of "What's wrong with this sentence?" (elbows don't kick, a soccer ball is too big for a thimble). Such adventures with sense and nonsense and logic and illogic in sentences help students make differentiations that will be important for their later understanding of all types of literacy materials. An exploration of logic will help them make distinctions between fiction and nonfiction, tabloid journalism and fact-based reporting, science fiction and science writing, rhetoric and reasoned argument, and creative writing and expository writing, among many other possibilities.

Using Logical Strategies in the Reading and Writing of Text

As mentioned earlier in this chapter, when students read they are like scientists trying to make sense of data. This becomes even more true when they are investigating whole chunks of text. Before students have even started reading the text, they must call upon a number of inner cognitive structures in deciding how to proceed. For example, "Is this a text that I'm going to be *able* to read?" Students also have to ask: "What sort of text am I getting myself into, anyway? Is this a novel? A story? Fiction? Nonfiction?" and then mentally go through the different genres and forms of literacy they are familiar with, so as to be able to put this current text into a context of familiarity. Or, conversely, they may need to put it into a context of unfamiliarity: "I've never seen a text like this before!" We've all had this kind of experience when encountering a new literary form for the first time, whether it be our first play, first science fiction story, a piece of avant garde poetry, or some other new or experimental genre or work. Readers also have to decide why they are reading. For pleasure? For a test? For a research project? The answer may determine whether the text is read word for word, for quick details, in a slow and leisurely manner, or in some other way. Such questions as those raised above come together to form a kind of informal, logical decision tree that for accomplished readers is sorted through almost instantaneously before sitting down to read a book.

While reading the text itself, students need to ask further questions. First and foremost is the big question, "What is this text mainly about?" Developing logical strategies, such as looking for a main idea early in the text or at the beginning of paragraphs, or looking at titles, subtitles, italicized phrases, or key phrases, such as "It is especially important that we understand . . . " can assist readers in more efficiently comprehending the essential meanings of the material (Goldman & Rakestraw, Jr., 2000). Taking in lots of different ideas or events (if it is a fictional work) in the course of a few pages, good readers must sort through this material and put it into some type of order or sequence. ("They robbed a bank, then hid out, then got caught, then escaped.") In addition, they need to ask themselves questions about key events ("How did they manage to escape from that high-security prison?"), identify contradictions that seem to be in the text ("It just said that Mr. Hughes was a police officer, but I thought he was one of the bad guys") and make tentative decisions to resolve these contradictions ("Maybe Hughes is a crooked cop . . . oh yah . . . maybe *he* had something to do with the breakout!"). Just like good scientists, accomplished readers are those who can keep asking themselves questions about the meaning of the text as they go along, creating little hypotheses to help resolve predicaments ("Maybe he's a crooked cop") and then confirming and disconfirming the hypotheses later on in the text. ("I guess he's not a crooked cop. It just said he caught one of the bad guys. Unless, maybe he was just trying to look good to the other cops.")

In writing text, similar sorts of guidelines hold true. "What kind of text (or genre) do I want to write? What is my purpose in writing this? What essential meanings do I want the reader to get from my text?" In formulating answers to these types of questions, the good writer is able to select the appropriate form (letter, story, poem, play, speech), and audience (my teacher, my peers, the readership of *Horn Book* magazine, myself), and then go about creating a format and sequence that delivers the message in the best possible way. If the piece is an expository writing assignment for school, then the writer is careful to create a coherent thesis early on in the piece, developing arguments for the thesis as she goes along, and supporting these with facts, quotations, citations, and other materials that are directly relevant to the content, and finally restating the thesis and coming to a conclusion. If the piece is a haiku, then other logical procedures apply, including the need to write only three lines with five, seven, and five syllables, respectively. If the student is writing for himself in a journal that no one else will ever see, then he is guided only by the rule that he be able to communicate the material to himself, and even conventional spellings, words, and sentence structure may be dispensed with. But even this is a kind of logical rule. Writers (and readers as well) can be helped through the use of logical graphic organizers, including 5W organizers (Who, What, When, Where, Why), time lines, and Venn diagrams, which help categorize, sequence, organize in hierarchies, or in other ways assist in the process of thinking through the material to be written or read (Marchand-Martella, Miller, & MacQueen, 1998).

Books and Other Literacy Materials for Logical Minds

There is a wide range of literacy materials that appeal to the logical-mathematical person who is still feeling somewhat tentative or cautious about anything that has to do with words (as opposed to numbers or logical concepts). The simplest of these materials are probably children's counting books, such as *Richard Scarry's Best Counting Book Ever* or the Dr. Seuss classic *One Fish Two Fish Red Fish Blue Fish*. These basic counting books can also be used for addition, subtraction, and sometimes multiplication and division, as well as other logical concepts like set theory. There are also number books that focus on one particular number, like Jane Mencure's *My Six Book*, or on very large numbers, like Dr. Seuss's *The 500 Hats of Bartholomew Cubbins*. Children's literature also explores more abstract mathematical concepts like factorials and combinations in *Anno's Mysterious Mutliplying Jar*, and the classic *Alice's Adventures in Wonderland*, which was written by Lewis Carroll, an Oxford logician. For a list of children's literature that touches on mathematical themes, see Gailey (1993) and Thiessen, Mathias, and Smith (1998). For older students, look for literacy materials that have meaningful numbers in them, or that provide opportunities for exploring logic and reasoning, such as:

- Sports statistics books or the sports page of a newspaper;
- Math texts in domains where students feel confident;

- Brainteaser books and magazines;
- Mystery stories and novels that provide clues that need to be solved;
- Cookbooks; and
- Repair manuals.

Also look at books that explore science themes, including both science fiction and real science materials. These might include books like *Anna to the Infinite Power* and *The Technology Book for Girls and Other Advanced Beings*. One of my personal favorites is Philip and Phylis Morrison's *Powers of Ten*, based on the Charles and Ray Eames film of the same name. Starting with a view of the entire universe, the book goes by successive powers of 10 down to a picnic by the shores of Lake Michigan, then focuses on a human hand, and in several more steps gets down to the subatomic particles in an atom. Some books come with attached materials for students to create their own scientific experiments, such as David Packard and Marshall H. Peck's book *Grow Your Own Crystals* or the Klutz Press book *ExploraBook: A Kids' Science Museum in a Book*.

Logical-Mathematical Literacy Styles

It's interesting to speculate about some of the habits of the highly logical-mathematical person when it comes to literacy. In addition to using some of the problem-solving and hypothesis-testing strategies, and the types of literacy materials described above, such a person might well be interested in the idea of literacy itself as a quantifiable process. Wise (2002), for example, suggests that students should be directly involved in the computation of the readability of a text by applying a simple readability formula to the texts that they are reading. This activity might particularly interest individuals with logical-mathematical proclivities, and it could make entering the world of books more appealing to them. Similarly, such students might be interested in keeping a log of the number of pages they have read, or the time they spend reading, or the number of books or other materials they have read over a given period of time. They might be interested in measuring their own reading speed or reading comprehension, or at least in having access to reading test results that are administered to them by others. They also might be interested in keeping track of the number of words they write over a given period of time (the "word count" feature on many word processing programs is ideally suited to this purpose). Finally, they might be interested in classifying or categorizing the material they read in various ways—for example, by genre (this month; only mysteries; next month, only science fiction) or readability (along a continuum from easiest to read to most difficult).

For Further Study

- Experiment with using different kinds of graphic organizers (Venn diagrams, 5W charts, etc.) to help students think about the sound-letter correspondences, words, sentences, and texts they are learning to read and write.

- Create a "Word Dissection Lab" modeled after a science laboratory, where students use actual lab tools (or safer substitutes) to cut up words into syllables or morphemes and analyze them under a magnifying glass or microscope. Include scientific-looking charts that offer rules for "word dissection" (e.g., word attack skills).

- Ask students to share the problem-solving processes they go through when reading something that they don't initially understand. Encourage them to articulate what questions, ideas, or strategies work best for them.

- Create an activity center or display area that provides "The History of Words." Each word might be put on a time line showing how its spelling, pronunciation, and meaning have changed over time.

6

Feeling the Emotional Power of Text

When I was a special education teacher at the elementary level, my students would frequently get into huge conflicts during recess and then carry their emotions into the classroom with them where they (the feelings) proceeded to disturb the learning process considerably. While the behavior modification program I used at the time usually was successful in coercing the kids back into their seats and focusing them on the material at hand, I never saw such dramatic results as when I began to ask them to *write* about the fights they were getting into out there on the playground. I told them that I wanted to hear everybody's point of view about what happened, but that I wanted it *in print*. As soon as I said this, I could almost see the emotional energy of my students switch directions and flow from their unsettled bodies through the pencils they gripped tightly in their hands onto the page in the form of coherent narratives ("Joey made me trip so I hit him and then the yard duty yelled at me"). That experience impressed on me the tremendous importance that human emotions have on literacy; that they are essentially, to quote Dylan Thomas, "the force that through

81

the green fuse drives the flower." Emotions fuel the desire to communicate with words.

Emotions color our very first experiences with literacy. I have to chuckle a little when I hear educators and researchers discuss reading and writing as if they were exact sciences. Perhaps they are for individuals with a logical-mathematical bent. But I suspect that for most of us, our early memories of literacy acquisition were probably not scientifically neutral experiences of learning simple correspondences between the sound "buh" and the letter *b*, or the blending of "puh" with "eh" and "tuh" to make the word *pet*. Instead, I'll bet these memories were something far more luminous, set in a complex web of emotions: sitting in the arms of a loved one reading a book together, angrily attempting to write some words after a real or imagined slight, writing a love note to a secret admirer, listening to a fairy tale before drifting off into dreamland. In his memoirs, Pablo Neruda, the Chilean poet and 1971 Nobel Prize winner in Literature, reminisced about one of his own early literacy experiences:

> Once, far back in my childhood, when I had barely learned to read, I felt an intense emotion and set down a few words, half rhymed but strange to me, different from everyday language. Overcome by a deep anxiety, something I had not experienced before, a kind of anguish and sadness, I wrote them neatly on a piece of paper . . . I had no way at all of judging my first composition, which I took to my parents . . . My father took it absentmindedly, read it absentmindedly and returned it to me absentmindedly saying, "where did you copy this from?" Then he went on talking to my mother in a lowered voice about his important and remote affairs. That, I seem to remember, was how my first poem was born (Neruda, 1977, p. 20).

Neruda's first writing experience was couched in painful emotions. But the discovery of literacy has its ecstatic moments as well. Maria Montessori writes about one such glorious day in Rome in 1907, when her 4- and 5-year-old students taught themselves to write:

> This was the greatest event to take place in the first Children's Home. The child who first made the discovery was so astonished

that he shouted out loud: "I've written, I've written!" The children excitedly ran up to look at the words which he had traced on the floor with a piece of chalk. "Me too, me too!" they shouted as they ran off in search of writing materials. Some crowded around the blackboard. Others stretched themselves out upon the floor. They all began to write. Their boundless activity was like a torrent. They wrote everywhere, on doors, walls, and even on loaves of bread at home (Montessori, 1973, pp. 131-132).

The vast majority of brain research studies in the field of reading and writing have tended to neglect the contribution of the emotions to literacy with their focus on the more straightforward aspects of phonological processing, lexical decoding, syntactic construction, and other technical matters. However, there is a small but growing literature that links reading and writing to areas of the brain that process emotions. Joseph (1992) writes about the involvement of the limbic system or "emotional brain" in the processing of language generally:

> Auditory information is received in the primary auditory area, as well as within the amygdala of the limbic system (and other limbic areas). Emotional and related characteristics are discerned, comprehended, and/or assigned to the sounds perceived. When one is speaking emotionally or is singing or cursing, this information is transferred from the temporal-parietal and limbic areas to the right frontal area, which mediates the expression of the information. (p. 80)

Similarly, the processing of emotionally charged *written* text takes place, in part, outside of the normal left-hemispheric circuits involved in phonology, syntax, and precise semantic identification of words. It appears, for example, that when an individual is attempting to decode an ambiguous word, the right hemisphere is involved in a process of making available to the reader a set of alternative word meanings (Coney & Evans, 2000). A reader who sees and then reads, for example, the word *rabbit* in a text, may also be processing a wide range of associated words (*bunny, foot, lucky charm, Bugs, furry, cage,* and so on) that aren't ever read, or even allowed into conscious awareness. This is consistent with the work of Freudian psychoanalysis, which investigates "slips of the tongue" as well as emotionally meaningful mistakes made during reading and writing. Freud himself was an avid collector of old objects, and he wrote that whenever he was walking on the streets of a strange city, he read the word *antiquities* on every shop sign that showed the slightest resemblance to the word (Freud, 1966). The psychoanalyst Bruno Bettelheim examined the reading errors of children with a view to deciphering their underlying emotional significance. For example, Bettelheim suggested that a 1st grade child who had misread the word *Tigger* for *tiger* might be substituting the tamer version of the Winnie-the-Pooh character in order to shy away from confronting the more dangerous animal/word (Bettelheim, 1981).

Another indication that there is a region in the brain in the right hemisphere that processes loose word associations comes from a condition known as "deep dyslexia." In deep dyslexia, the reader makes mistakes that are semantically related in some way to the correct word. For example, in place of reading the word *whiskey*, the reader might read the word *spirit* (we sometimes call different types of alcoholic beverages *spirits*). This suggests that the left hemisphere has recognized and decoded the correct word but that the right hemisphere has substituted an alternative word in its place (Michel, Hanaff, & Intrillgator, 1996). In other studies, aphasic patients were shown to be able to read emotional words better than nonemotional words by using intact right hemispheric functions (Landis, Graves, & Goodglass, 1982), and children identified as dyslexic were better able to read anxiety-laden words than words with a more neutral content (Van Strien, Stolk, & Zuiker, 1995). It's rather telling, in passing, to note that research in the field of dyslexia (Shaywitz et al., 1998) indicates that the one linguistic area that "dyslexic subjects" have the most difficulty with is in reading nonsense words that rhyme. In other words, they have the most trouble reading words bereft of meaning, and thus, one would suspect, of any real emotional connection. Clearly, the right hemisphere and underlying limbic system structures also have another part to play in the literacy process in the way that they govern the emotional responses to words and texts.

Young children and great writers don't need to be familiar with the brain research literature in order to know the connection between words and emotions. Werner (1973) describes a four-year-old girl who says about her father: "Father talks just like Santa Claus . . . boom,

boom, boom! As dark as night . . . ! But we talk light, like the daytime . . . bim, bim, bim!" In one experiment, Werner asked children aged 7 to 10 to write the words *scared* and *joy*, noting that the kids naturally tended to write the word *scared* in tightly squashed letters (affectively reflecting its meaning), while using a more expansive and rounded script to represent the word *joy* (Werner, 1973, pp. 264-265). On the other end of the literacy continuum, Shakespeare was constantly reveling in the experience of emotions in his text. Witness, for example, the venting of aggression through his famous insults: "[Thou hath] not so much brain as ear wax" (*Troilus and Cressida*); and "[Thine] horrid image doth unfix my hair" (*Macbeth*). Samuel Johnson, the originator of the first systematic dictionary of the English language, loaded his word entries with humorous affective tones, for example, defining *lexicographer*, in part, as "a writer of dictionaries; a harmless drudge" (McAdam & Milne, 1995). And American poet James Merrill once remarked that the real way to express life's events isn't in a linear order, like "See Jane run." Rather it's far more natural to express the event dynamically and emotionally: "Where on earth can that child be racing off to? Why, it's little—you know, the neighbor's brat—Jane!" (McClatchy, 1995).

Putting Some Feeling into Teaching Letters and Sounds

I spoke earlier in the chapter about the emotionally neutral way in which all too many children learn letter-sound correspondences in standard reading programs (*b* makes the sound "buh," say "buh"; *p* makes the sound "puh," say "puh," and so on). It certainly doesn't need to be that way. In fact, if you look at the approximately 44 phonemes of the English language, these sounds connect to many different types of emotions that we feel every day. For example, the "oo" sound in *boot* is also a sound we make when we see something that's pretty exciting: "Oooooo . . . that's a great bike you've got there!" The "ai" sound in *bait* (or "ay" sound in *stay*), reminds me of the television show *Happy Days*, when Fonzie would express his coolness by raising his thumbs and exclaiming "Ayyyyy!" When I taught first generation Portuguese students in Montreal, Canada, they would often express displeasure with the "ee" sound: "Eeeeee, Sir! Why do we have to do all this homework?"

The "oy" in *boy* is a common Yiddish expression ("Oy, what a day I've had"). We could probably go on down the line, finding emotional connections to most of the phonemes in the English language.

Once students have anchored each phoneme in a specific emotional expression (perhaps accompanied by an appropriate physical posture, as in the Fonzie example), then their ability to discriminate between them, and to relate them to specific letters and letter combinations is likely to improve, given the fact that these are no longer meaningless sounds disconnected from their lives, but rather vital expressions of feeling. Similarly, the process of sound blending can become far more exuberant than it generally is in standard reading programs ("say buh-ah-llll . . . ball"), if the blends represent emotionally charged words. On the old *Batman* television program, when Batman and Robin would engage in combat with an archenemy, various "word explosions" would appear on the screen to describe the actions taking place, words such as: *Bonk! Scrunch! Splat! Blat! Gong! Batz!* I would suggest that students have a far greater likelihood of success in blending when using these emotionally charged words, rather than when they interact with the affectively flat words found in most standard reading programs.

It's also possible to bring an emotional quality to letters by giving them physiognomic characteristics. Child development researcher Heinz Werner defines physiognomic perception as follows:

> All of us, at some time or other, have had this experience. A landscape, for instance, may be seen suddenly in immediacy as expressing a certain mood—it may be gay or melancholy or pensive. This mode of perception differs radically from the more everyday perception in which things are known according to their "geometrical-technical," matter-of-fact qualities, as it were. In our own sphere there is one field where objects are commonly perceived as directly expressing an inner life. This is in our perception of the faces and bodily movements of human beings and higher animals. Because the human physiognomy can be adequately perceived only in terms of its immediate expression, I have proposed the term physiognomic perception for this mode of cognition in general (Werner, 1973, p. 69).

Werner uses the example of the letter *L* (see Figure 6.1) drawn with a curve in the lower part of the letter that reaches out and "beckons" the way a human arm might. Such a letter acquires a certain emotional value to the perceiver. Educators can provide students with access to such "emotional alphabets" by creating their own versions, having an artist create them, letting the students develop their own lively alphabets, or acquiring creative alphabet books (see for example, Suse MacDonald's *Alphabatics*). Because visual print has tended to cut us *all* off from the emotional and dynamic qualities of oral speech (see Logan, 1986 and McLuan, 1965), anything we can do to get a little of it back by "emotionalizing" the alphabet will be especially helpful to those individuals who particularly suffer from its absence.

Figure 6.1

A Letter with Physiognomic Characteristics

Getting Emotional with Words

One of the best approaches to word acquisition that acknowledges the important role of emotions in literacy is Sylvia Ashton-Warner's "organic reading" method (Ashton-Warner, 1986). Ashton-Warner worked with Maori children in New Zealand, and realized that the textbooks being used to teach them contained language that was cut off from their own culture and personal world, so she asked students for their own words. The students offered up words such as *ghost*, *kill*, *grandmother*, and *kiss*. These were words that were not in the official reading program, but were words toward which the students had an emotional connection. Ashton-Warner had them keep their words in their personal index file for use in a variety of writing and reading activities.

Rico (1983) used the technique of "clustering" to help students generate nonlinear associations and ideas for writing. In clustering, students put a nucleus word or phrase in the center of a piece of paper and then free associate, with words radiating from the center (see Figure 6.2). These words can then be used creating a poem, building a story, writing an article, or creating other literacy projects. Such an approach is also useful for working with unfamiliar words. Students can, for example, take the week's vocabulary list and cluster around each word, creating word associations that will help them remember the word and relate it to other words and personal or emotional associations and images (see Figure 6.3).

Figure 6.2

A Middle School Student's Mind-Map for the Word *Lonely*

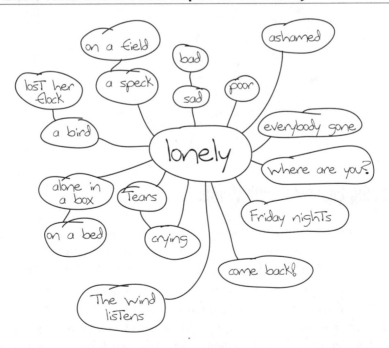

Here are some other ways educators can help students work with individual words in ways that use the emotions:

- Take each word on a spelling list and spell it "cheerleader style" with lots of feeling: "Give me a G! G! Give me an R! R! Give me an E! E! Give me another E! E! Give me an N! N! What does it spell? GREEN!!"

- Use word lists of emotions: happy, sad, jealous, joyful, jubilant, envious. Have students describe (or write about) incidents in their lives when they had an experience of each one.

- Let students create their own "invented" spellings for words as they write, without being bothered about correct orthography, so that the feeling and meaning of what they have to say will take precedence over mechanics.

- Have students create their own "emotion words" for use in writing assignments. "I'm really feeling flumbuxated right now!"

Figure 6.3

A High School Student's Mind-Map of the Word *Rambunctious*

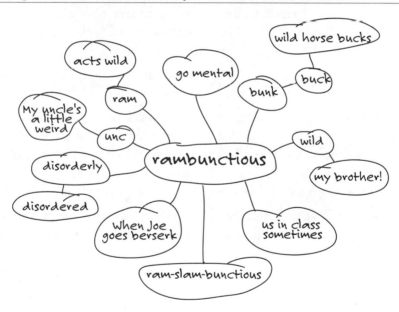

Reading and Writing Sentences with Feeling

When students who are emotionally sensitive are working with individual sentences in reading and writing activities, they ought to be emotionally engaged in the process, and not simply working with affectively flat sentences such as: "The cat sat on the mat" or "See Jane run." Sentences ought to reflect their own lives and personal experiences: "*My* cat Scooter sat on *our* bathroom mat." Or "See *my friend* Rhonda run." If one has to work with the standard reading program material, at least spice up the words with some strong emotional inflections in the voice. When teaching students, avoid the monotone voice, even in simple and boring reading program sentences—put some life into it! Here are a number of other ways to punch up emotional content when working with sentence meaning and structure:

- Have students write sentences that begin with "I," "My," or "Our" and allow them to reveal something of their own lives and feelings in the process: "My dog Ralphie pooped on the carpet. I felt bad."

- Work with emotion verbs in constructing and reading new sentences. For example, have them create sentences with the two verbs *love* and *hate*: "I love apple pie. I hate getting slugged in the arm."

- Let them create sentences that include their own name, names of friends or family, and personal possessions.

- Use humor in writing funny sentences. For example, have students write sentences that have intentionally poor grammar ("I is going at the moon") or illogical syntax, such as using nouns for verbs and vice versa ("He groceried to the went") and after the laughs subside, explore what's wrong with the syntax.

- Encourage students to put extra emotional intonation into reading sentences that have an exclamation mark or a question mark (and suggest that they note the different sort of emotional intonations one uses for each of these punctuation marks).

Reading and Writing with Passion

When it comes to reading comprehension skills, teachers often seem to me far more interested in whether students can apply critical thinking skills to the text than in whether they actually *care* about the material they are reading. I sometimes like to ask educators in my workshops to choose the better student in a reading class: one who can tell you the main idea of a story or novel, plot the sequence, make inferences, predict outcomes, and summarize accurately, or one who feels pity or sadness when the main character in the story confronts an obstacle, or rejoices when the protagonist triumphs over adversity. Naturally school culture favors the first student, but I believe a lifetime of literacy favors the second reader. We read to more deeply experience life, the world, and ourselves. Franz Kafka once wrote that a book should serve as "the ax for the frozen sea inside us" (letter to Oskar Pollak, January 27, 1904). It should stir us inside, loosen the compacted soil of our fixed attitudes and stereotypes, and transform the way we think and live. The writer Harold Brodkey noted that "in Europe, reading is known to be dangerous. Reading almost always leads to personal metamorphosis, sometimes irreversible, sometimes temporary, sometimes large-scale . . . . A good book leads to alterations in one's sensibility and often becomes a premise in one's beliefs" (Brodkey, 1985, p. 44).

What are we doing in our literacy programs, reading classes, and literature courses to help students feel deeply what they read? We need to remember that while illiteracy is a terrible plague on society, so is *aliteracy*, a term I like to use to describe people who are *able* to read, but *choose* not to do so. Too many people are turned off by text because they feel there is nothing in the words that speaks to their lives, their concerns, their hopes and dreams. What can educators do to help? Here are some ideas:

- Select material for reading that has been passionately written. Avoid textbook materials that have been written by committees or with a "school culture" voice.

- Include genres as texts that especially lend themselves to emotional expression, such as poetry, plays, novels, dialogues, monologues, love letters, and romances.

- Allow space in the classroom for students to respond openly with emotions to material they are reading—let them know, for example, that it's okay to cry, or laugh, or respond in some other appropriate way if the material moves them.

- Transcribe a student's oral descriptions of his or her own life for use as text in reading activities.

- When you read stories and novels to your students, put passion into your delivery. Even now, 40 years later, I can still feel inside the emotions of one of my elementary school teachers,

Miss Opperman, as she read from *Island of the Blue Dolphins.* Give your own students something like that to remember you by 40 years from now.

- As students read text, ask them periodically to share what emotions are brought up by the material, and discuss these feelings with them in a sensitive and caring way.

- Ask students to share what they think the characters in the story are feeling, and what the author might have been feeling when he wrote the work.

Similarly, in writing activities, help students move beyond the superficial mechanics of writing to focus on what real writers care most about: telling a moving story in the most compelling way possible and revealing something deep and unique about the self, the world, and life. Use writing themes that encourage passionate or emotional exploration (for example, The Saddest Thing in Life, My Dream for the World, A Romance that Never Died, The Loneliest Part of the Day). Try Rico's (1983) clustering technique using emotion words as a starting point in writing poems or creative stories that allow the inner self to speak out loud. Encourage students to write about their dreams, desires, hopes, and fears (see Koch, 1970). Let them keep personal journals that are free from evaluation and teacher monitoring. Give them regular free-writing times when they can write about whatever comes into their hearts and minds.

Books and Other Literacy Materials That Evoke Feelings

In choosing books and other literacy materials that will evoke feelings in the reader, let me first say that any *great* fiction writer qualifies, whether it be someone as cerebral as Jorge Luis Borges, as deeply sensitive as Virginia Woolf, or as sentimental as Charles Dickens. Beyond this, and especially for children, there are a number of book genres that are particularly suited to making connections with the emotional world. First, there are books that deal explicitly with feelings, such as *Feeling Angry*, or the series *I'm Excited, I'm Frustrated,* and *I'm Furious,* as well as classic children's books such as Judith Viorst's *Alexander and the Terrible, Horrible, No Good, Very Bad Day.* Second, there are books that help children deal with special problems like separation or divorce, violence, illness, death of family members, and other issues that bring up deep emotions (Tu, 1999). Such books include *Losing Uncle Tim,* which is about a boy's loss of his uncle to AIDS, or *Good-Bye, Daddy!* where a child's teddy bear helps him cope with his parents' divorce. Third, there are books that deal with emotionally charged themes such as racism and sexual abuse. These books include Laurie Halse Anderson's *Speak,* about a high school freshman's rape, and *Sounder,* by William Howard Armstrong, which deals with racism in the South. Also in this category are books that have been banned because they have raised controversial subjects that special interest groups have sought to suppress. These books include Maya Angelou's *I Know Why the Caged Bird Sings* and *Are You There God? It's Me, Margaret* by Judy Blume. Fourth, one should keep in mind blank books that allow the writer/reader to write their own text. For example, Klutz Press publishes a *Dream Journal* that includes information about recording dreams and has special prompts to help writers put down their own nighttime reveries.

Literacy Styles of the Emotionally Sensitive

For individuals whose emotional sensitivity is part of their literacy, it's important to let them explore reading and writing without the traditional shackles of regimented and lockstep programs, worksheets, and skill books. Emphasis should be placed on letting them choose their own books or texts. As much as possible, such readers should own their books rather than borrow them from a library or use the school's texts. They can then write in them (venting emotional comments to the characters or author in the margins), talk back to them, and even throw them down on the ground if they happen to disagree with a writer's point of view (although we'll hope that they don't damage their books irreparably). They should have frequent opportunities for unstructured writing in diaries and personal journals, where they can record dreams, poetry, reflections, reveries, visions, or other revelations of their inner life (and these should not be part of the evaluation process, or even necessarily read by the teacher). Ideally, such individuals should be allowed, whenever possible, to go off and write at any time of the day when the writing Muse strikes them. Also, their own idiosyncratic writing rituals should be honored as much as possible. Hemingway used to sharpen his pencils to help him get in the mood. The German poet Schiller kept a drawer full of rotten apples to give him inspiration. John Keats dressed up in formal wear before he sat down to write a poem (Lopate, 1977). Help students discover whatever it takes to get them in the mood to read and write. Finally, make sure that you approach literacy on a daily basis as an adventure in self-discovery and self-development.

For Further Study

- Examine the reading and writing errors that students make with an eye to deciphering whether some of these errors may have been "Freudian slips" revealing unconscious emotions, attitudes, or images (for example, a student who reads the word *kill* for *kiss* or who writes *fury* for *funny*). Don't attempt to psychoanalyze the mistakes or the students, but explore the possibility that underneath a student's experiences with reading and writing, there are powerful undercurrents of words and word streams that represent attitudes and associations that aren't part of the conscious, conventional world. Work with genres of writing that are particularly well suited to loosening up those associations (e.g., poetry, short story writing).

- Develop with your students a phonics program that takes each of the 44 phonemes of English (or those that students have particular trouble with) and ties it to a particular emotional expression (and perhaps to a physical gesture as well—see Chapter 2). When doing word attack with the student during the reading of text, use these "emotional-kinesthetic phonemes" to help prompt them as to the correct sound value of a letter or group of letters (for example, use Fonzie's "Ayyyy!" to prompt for words like *eight*, *play*, *bait*, or *tape*).

- Create a writing time during the day when students are able to write freely on any subject, without being graded, and without having to show anyone what they've written. Talk with students about what it's like for them to be able to write under these freer conditions.

- Set up a center in your classroom related to "Words and Emotions." Perhaps this could be a center that students might go to when they have strong feelings that are interfering with the regular school activities, and where they can write about what's bothering them, thereby directing their energies in a constructive direction (this area should not be used as a time-out center having punitive associations). Or, alternatively, the center might focus on a specific emotion where students write and post poetry, stories, and other writings having to do with that specific feeling (e.g. "The Emotion of the Week: Fear").

7

Relating to the Social Context of Literacy

In his renowned autobiography, African American statesman and reformer Frederick Douglass wrote about his upbringing as a slave and his struggles in learning how to read and write at a time in America when a black person could be killed for attempting to become literate. He said that his most successful strategy as a youngster was to befriend little white boys he met on the street and enlist their aid in teaching him how to read. Douglass wrote: "With their kindly aid, obtained at different times and in different places, I finally succeeded in learning to read. When I was sent on errands, I always took my book with me, and by doing one part of my errand quickly, I found time to get a lesson before my return. I used also to carry bread with me . . . . This bread I used to bestow upon the hungry little urchins, who, in return, would give me that more valuable bread of knowledge" (Douglass, 1997, pp. 51–2). As Douglass became literate, he began to read books about slavery and its oppressiveness, started to articulate his own vision of a free society, and eventually escaped his bonds to become a key figure in the abolitionist movement and the emancipation of American slaves.

The experience of Frederick Douglass raises important issues about the role of literacy in social liberation. In the absence of any adult teacher (his owner had initially introduced him to the alphabet, but then, hardened by the racism of the times, blocked his attempts to read and write), Douglass used what today we would call "peer teaching" to becoming literate. He looked around him for alternative sources of support, and by understanding the social context of his times (little white boys could read, even if they lacked bread to eat), he used his own interpersonal skills to make teachers of these "hungry little urchins." Then, as he began to read books, his awareness of his own oppression deepened, fueling his desire to break out of a crippling social system and to create a more just society for himself and for others. Society, then, was a major key in both the suppression and in the subsequent acquisition of literacy for Douglass, and literacy, in turn, became an important instrument for him in the transformation of society.

All too often in today's individualistic society it seems that educators ignore the essential role of social context in teaching reading and writing. While no one would argue with the proposition that literacy makes students better citizens, the process of teaching reading and writing is still regarded by many as a didactic skill taught to *individual* students in a neutral and scientific way. Each student's literacy is defined in terms of an "objective" individual reading or writing level (Shari is reading at the 2.7 grade level; Bobby writes at a 4 level of mastery), and their personal reading and writing progress is often plotted on seemingly culture-free/culture-fair charts and graphs. Moreover, the ultimate social goals of literacy (Why do we want students to be able to read and write?) are oftentimes not explored in much depth, beyond such generalities as "so they can pass the high-stakes tests," "to communicate better with others," or "to gain knowledge of the world."

It is impossible to isolate literacy from its social context. Even the so-called scientific data-graphs and charts used in plotting reading and writing progress or in doing reading research—reveal much about the social context in which they are embedded. For one thing, they reveal that we live in a society where numbers are valued over common wisdom. Words owe their very existence to complex social factors. Each word is the product of a long series of negotiations between peoples within different social milieus. Take a look at the definitions of any word listed in the *Oxford English Dictionary*, and note how its meaning, pronunciation, and spelling have transformed themselves over the course of decades or centuries because of social factors. Words that were once considered to be highbrow, such as the words *moron* and *idiot* (used in the medical profession as diagnostic terms in the 1930s) only a few years later were transformed into lowbrow insults. In a sense, words are like money. They have value and specific meanings only if enough people agree that they do. Let's say, for example, that I wanted to have my own made-up word *stwart* replace the word *dog* as a description of that canine creature that is man's best friend. If I was able to run around the English-speaking world and get enough people to agree with me that *stwart* meant dog, then it would! Fortunately, or unfortunately as the case may be, I am unlikely to meet with much success in this effort. Yet new words are constantly being created within different social contexts—among steelworkers, punk rock musicians, e-zine journalists, government employees, and adolescent snowboarders.

What we know about language and literacy acquisition supports the view of words as a social phenomenon. We know that young children of different language backgrounds who have been thrown together by chance will create their own language from their interactions during play (Bickerton, 1982). Research suggests that children are more likely to develop emergent literacy skills through close friendships than through more distant peer relationships (Pellegrini, Galda, Bartini, & Charak, 1998). As individuals read, they must interpret words and sentences within an interpersonal context. What does the author (or character) really mean? A sentence reads: "John is a soldier." Does this mean that he belongs to the military? Or does it mean that he just has a strong personality? Or is someone making fun of John?

Because written text lacks all of the nonverbal information accessible to two individuals who communicate directly face to face, the reader (and writer) must call upon context, and use pragmatic and empathetic decision-making processes in order to make appropriate and meaningful interpretations of the written word (Sperber & Wilson, 2002). There are indications that such "mind reading" (deciphering the intentions of others) depends upon certain very specific neural mechanisms in the brain, and that such skills are fundamental to the acquisition of linguistic competence in young children (Vogeley et al., 2001; Meltzoff, 1999). Nobody invents a language, creates a book, coins a word, or utters a meaningful sentence as a single individual operating within a cultural vacuum. All of this linguistic activity takes place within a rich social milieu.

At the same time, when new language is invented, when a book is written, when a word is coined, or when a sentence is uttered, society changes along with it. The young child observes and participates in the *power* of words. This is a muscular power, as noted in Chapter 2, but it is also a *social power*. An infant says the word "up" and suddenly the social environment around her changes; it enfolds itself around her and moves her into contact with people. An 8-year-old writes the words "Go Away!" on a piece of paper and tacks it to his bedroom door, and suddenly he shapes the social world around him in a tangible way that powerfully expresses the temporary distance he wishes to have with respect to that world. A 6th grader writes an essay on environmental waste that helps to create a recycling program for her school. A teenager writes a passionate love letter to a girl he just met and discovers to his joy that it serves to transform an accidental meeting into a significant romantic relationship. An adult writes an article for a local newspaper on recent layoffs in his community and generates a political action group from among several of its unemployed readers. As noted in the introduction to this book, literacy has always been associated with power, whether it be political power, economic power, or civic power. On its most grand scale, words have transformed civilization itself. Look, for example, at the immeasurable impact of the following literary works on social history: the *Bible*, the *Koran*, Martin Luther's *95 Theses*, Karl Marx's *The Communist Manifesto*, Darwin's *Origin of Species*, and *Quotations from Chairman Mao Tse-Tung*.

Naturally, there is no assurance that words will always change society in a dramatic way. The infant may howl the word "up" until she is blue in the face, and no one may come. The school child may write the environmental essay, only to have it filled with red pencil marks and given a *D* for poor penmanship. The teenager may strike out with both the letter and the girl. The adult may find his submissions to periodicals met with rejection at every turn. In these cases, each individual may begin to suspect the *impotence* of words. Sadly, much of education today seems to reinforce this view, by requiring students over the course of 12 or more years of study to write thousands of pages of written material that has no broad social purpose—no mini-revolutions to foment, no big or small social reforms to create, no cultural transformations to effect—but rather serve only the very narrowest social goal of "doing what the teacher wants me to do." When students feel that their words are written only to be graded and then tossed into the wastepaper basket, then clearly they are being indoctrinated into the social impotence of words. This chapter focuses instead on helping students realize how words can function to broaden and transform their social worlds.

Developing a Critical Phonics Program

One of the problems with traditional phonics programs is that they lack any fundamental connection to a significant social context. The sound "buh" is connected to the letter *b*, but this pairing has no relevance to the social world of the student (and may only reinforce her opinion that the social world of adult teachers is a rather alien world). The Brazilian educator Paulo Freire recognized the vital importance of linking literacy acquisition to the meaningful social, economic, and political worlds of his students, and his phonetic system reflected this broad cultural focus. After much preparatory work in helping his students understand the power of literacy to transform themselves and society, he used words for phonetic analysis that came directly from their social milieu. So, for example, with adult workers who were just learning to read, he used the word *brick* (*tijolo* in Portuguese), since it was vitally connected to their work life as laborers at construction sites. This word was broken into syllables: *ti-jo-lo*, and then its various vowel combinations were generated: *ta-te-ti-to-tu*; *ja-je-ji-jo-ju*, and *la-le-li-lo-lu*. Students would then recombine these syllables to make other word combinations (for example, *tatu*—armadillo; *luta*—struggle). Out of around 17 such generative words, students would create thousands of additional word combinations to read and write (Freire, 1998).

While this system is not easily transferred to English because English lacks the consistent vowel-rich, short-syllabic structure of the Portuguese language, Freire's basic principles can nevertheless be applied in English-speaking classrooms. In such an approach, words used in phonetic discourse need to come directly from the social world of the students, and with their active collaboration. What are the words that are important in the social world of a 1st grader? A "dyslexic" teenager? A migrant farm worker just learning to read? In each case, the raw material for a phonetic program would be different. For example, socially significant words for 1st graders might include *candy*, *play*, *hit*, *love*, and *friend*. Out of these words, one might isolate the syllables *-an*, *-end*, *-lay*, and *-it*, and then generate new word combinations from them: *man*, *can*, *tan*; *bend*, *lend*, *tend*; *lay*, *pay*, *say*; and *fit*, *lit*, and *bit*. The important thing is that the basis of learning phonetic sounds must emerge, not from the research culture of a systematic but externally imposed phonics program, but rather from the socially relevant language used by the students. Similarly, in learning the alphabet, rather than linking each letter to a word that is arbitrarily chosen by the worksheet manufacturer or the alphabet book author, teachers can create with the students an alphabet based upon words that are socially significant to them. For example, with a group of teenagers labeled as "severely dyslexic": *A* is for *awesome*, *B* is for *basketball*, *C* is for *cool*. Here are some other ways to make learning letters and letter-sound correspondences a social event:

- Let each student become an expert in one or two of the phonetic sounds of the English language, which she can then teach to other students. For example, one student may be an expert in the "ay" in *play*. He would know the sound, and also its various visual equivalents (the "ai" in *bait*, the "a" in *gate* and so on), and could tutor his classmates accordingly. Another student may be the "oo" expert.

- Once students have mastered their individual sounds, they can then begin to come together as "people blends." For example, the "t" expert might get together with the "oo" expert, and the "l" expert and blend their sounds together to make the word *tool* (or *loot*). This game could even work like musical chairs, with kids walking around making their sounds, and at a signal from the teacher, each student could link arms with two other students and work out (or attempt to work out) a blended word.

- To work on specific letter sounds, choose four or five phonemes, and go around and whisper one or another of them into the ear of every student. Then, at a signal, students must make their letter sound, and mill about the room, finding all the others who are making the same sound.

- Give each student a letter of the alphabet (mix up the order). Then have the class organize themselves in alphabetical order.

- Form letters of the alphabet from groups of students (for example, have five people lie on the ground to make an *A*). Then take pictures of each "letter group" from a bird's-eye view, and make these photos the "class alphabet."

Getting Social with Words

As students learn new vocabulary words in school, it's very important that they incorporate them immediately into their social world. Too often, students master word lists only to satisfy the requirements of "school culture" or "test culture." They'll use the traditional school methods for studying the words—making flash cards, using the words in a sentence, and looking them up in the dictionary. Once the test results are in, or the grade achieved, these words are then discarded from their lives. To counter this common pattern, teachers need to focus on helping students use their vocabulary words in their everyday speech, and in as many different "mini-cultures" as possible. Encourage them to use the words not just during official class discussions, but also informally with friends, other teachers, parents, younger students, and people in the community. To initiate this process, a teacher might take the 15 vocabulary words for the week, and begin introducing them into *her* speech patterns while she gives instructions, lectures, or makes small talk before or after class. Each student might then be given one or more vocabulary words to use as much as possible during the day (in school, among peers, and at home). Finally, students can come back to class the next day and discuss the social experiences involved in using the new words.

Here are a few other ways to make word study (and spelling) more social:

- Ask students to teach the week's vocabulary list to younger students. This approach is based on an expression in Latin: *Qui docet discet*, meaning: "One who teaches, learns."

- Choose words to learn (and discuss) that have particular social importance, or trigger strong social responses, such as *race*, *patriot*, *terrorist*, and *abortion*.

- Examine the social history of specific word origins using the *Oxford English Dictionary*, or a book on word origins such as John Ayto's *Dictionary of Word Origins*. For example, the word *boycott* was named after Captain Charles Cunningham Boycott, a British estate manager who was *boycotted* in 1880 by the Irish Land League as a way of asserting Irish autonomy over their own land.

- Give each student a letter of the alphabet on a large colored card, and then go through this week's spelling list one by one, asking students who have the letters in each word to come up to the front of the class and assemble themselves with their cards held high, shouting the spelling in unison (use extra students to fill in with letters that repeat).

- Hold spelling bees and "vocabulary bees" on a regular basis, and encourage students to get involved in local, regional, and national contests.

Making Sentences Socially Relevant

When working with individual sentences and sentence construction, use sentences that are directly relevant to the interpersonal worlds of the students. This does not mean merely concocting artificial sentences that have a general social context ("The boys refused to play soccer with the girls"), but rather using sentences from the real worlds of the actual students involved. Of course, a great deal of sensitivity is required here. It would be a gross violation of student privacy, and of group dynamics in general, to take a bit of juicy gossip ("Joey thinks Susan is cute") and make it a subject for grammar study (unless all the parties involved give the okay). On the other hand, it certainly makes sense to create sentences out of more descriptive, and thus less controversial, aspects of the students' social world: "John plays football on Tuesday afternoons with Peter and Raddo." "Wendy had lunch yesterday with Rhonda and Maria." These sentences can become the starting point for looking at various grammatical points. For example, Wendy is now not only someone we know personally, but she is also the subject of a sentence. Peter and Raddo are part of a prepositional phrase. John and Wendy each have their own verb. It's important for the teacher to be playfully interactive with the students as she works with these types of sentences ("I understand that Wendy *would have had* lunch with Ellie, too, but she was sick yesterday. Isn't that so, Wendy? And, you *shall have* lunch with whom today?").

Reading and Writing as Social Action

As students begin to read text, they should also start reflecting, in however simple a way, on what it means to be reading text as a literate person living in given society at a specific moment in history. Emerging readers are not automatons, passively receiving printed words from books and blackboards, and then mechanically processing the text. Instead they are active participants in their own emerging literacy and ought to be treated accordingly. An entire field of *critical literacy* has emerged over the past several years, inspired in part by the work of Paulo Freire, which is dedicated to encouraging dialogue and reflection about what it means to be literate, what it's like to experience different kinds of texts, how texts reflect societal values, and how texts can transform society (Creighton, 1997; Macrine, 1997; Ludwig & Herschell, 1998; McCall & Ford, 1998; Comber, Thomson, & Wells, 2001).

Students need to learn that there are many different kinds of texts, and that each text is uniquely embedded in a societal context. There is text in library books, text on television, text in high-stakes tests, text on the blackboard, text on a cafeteria menu. And each of these texts differ in their social purposes and aims. Kids intuitively suspect, for example, that there is something very different about the text in a phonics workbook as compared with the text in a classic children's literature storybook. But it's up to the educator to help students make these distinctions explicit. It may be far more important to talk about these differences than to fill in the correct blanks on the phonics worksheet or give the main idea of the storybook. Some questions to consider in dialogue with students: Where did this text come from? (students may think that text, like meat in a supermarket, comes to us prewrapped from some centralized place). What do you think the author wants you to think about the text? What do *you* think about as you read the text? How is this text (e.g., children's literature) different from this other text (e.g., advertising in a newspaper)? I am alarmed by the fact that students are exposed to enormous quantities of marketing-oriented media text during much of their time out of school, from ads on television to trademarks on sneakers and slogans on billboards, and yet no one is there in an educational role to help them think about these texts. Students need a chance to talk about what advertisements mean, how they operate, who writes them, and what purpose they serve.

Even within a particular genre, such as children's storybooks, there are social issues crying out to be explored. What happens when black students, for example, are exposed primarily to children's literature written from a white perspective? Or when girls read literature peopled solely with male protagonists? A student may wonder: "Why isn't *my* social world being reflected in anything that I'm reading? I'm a Sioux teenager living in rural South Dakota, but they're having me read books about white children living in Manhattan skyscrapers and London townhouses!" These types of reactions need to be made explicit in the classroom through dialogue between students and the teacher. Questions to explore in text: How does this text speak or not speak to you personally? How does it reflect or not reflect your social world? How does it raise questions for you about the ways in which people of a different race, gender, ethnic group, religion, or sexual orientation live?

Over the past three decades, much educational text has been infused with multicultural themes and alternative lifestyles. However, additional critical questions might include: How authentic are these texts? Have they been written merely to satisfy a climate of political correctness, or do they genuinely mirror the diversity of our culture? Finally, an additional theme that might be explored is censorship. What texts do certain groups not want students to read? What are their reasons for this? Is this fair in a society that values and defends free speech? These questions, and others like them (adjusted, of course, to the developmental level of the students) should be considered an important part of acquiring literacy at any age.

Similarly, when involving students in the writing of text, social issues ought to play an important role. Are students merely doing a writing assignment to fulfill an academic requirement, or is the text written to make a difference in the social world beyond the classroom? Students need to feel from their earliest writing experience that their words can make a difference in the world. Some of their earliest writing should be in the form of letters or e-mail to influential people or periodicals or organizations, stating points of view, requesting information, sharing valuable insights, or providing their own unique ideas for changing society.

We should treat students learning to write like real writers. Instead of "English class" or "remedial writing," we ought instead to create "writer's workshops" where kids can read and discuss their own work in a professional manner. Or educators might set up "publishing seminars" where kids can learn to plan writing projects, and then go through each step of the process in taking their projects to final completion in the form of a finished pamphlet, bound manuscript, Web site, or handmade book. We need to encourage students, and not just the so-called gifted ones, to submit their projects to appropriate literary sources, whether it be the class newsletter, the school newspaper, the "letters to the editor" section of the community newspaper, a children's poetry review, or a full-fledged publishing house (even a rejection slip is an affirmation of sorts that one is a *real* writer trying to make it in the highly competitive world of publishing). Here are a number of other ways to infuse the social world into the process of reading and writing:

- Let students correspond with pen pals or "key pals" (via e-mail) around the world.

- Have students collaborate on a writing project. Point out to them that most scientific papers are written collaboratively, sometimes by as many as 10 or 15 people.

- Ask each student what his or her favorite social cause is, and then plan with them a writing project that will promote it in some way, such as a letter-writing campaign, text for a public display, or a submission to a newspaper or journal.

- Have groups of students "jigsaw" several reading assignments, where each member of a small group will read one portion of their assignment and report to the other members. Then, each group can report to the whole class about their piece.

- During class discussions of texts, ask students questions designed to guide them into the minds of the author or characters. For example, ask: "What was the author's intent in writing this piece?" or "What do you think the main character intended to do at this point?"

- Encourage students to enter writing contests, do poetry readings, or engage in other events where their writing will be read in a public setting.

Books for Socially Conscious People

As noted above, it's important to provide students with books that mirror their own social worlds, including religious, ethnic, racial, gender, and sexual preference identifications. For a list of multicultural children's literature see Steiner (2001); for books written specifically for boys or girls, see Odean (1997, 1998); for books for lesbian and gay youth (or children of lesbian or gay parents) see Day (2000). Then there are books that are themselves particularly accessible to group reading or interaction, including poster-sized Big Books such as *Flower Garden* by Eve Bunting and the Oxford University Press series *Poetry for Sharing*, which are large enough to be displayed and read by whole groups of students. Also in this category are board game books, such as *The Book of Classic Board Games* by Klutz Press, which includes laminated pages of board games from around the world, and game pieces, so that readers can gather around the book and play. Such books become magnets for social interaction. Dramatic plays, screenplays, and radio plays are also particularly well suited for social reading, as different students can take on particular parts. Books that include substantial dialogue between characters, especially when the dialogue is regional or involves dialects or varieties of English such as Black English, provide wonderful opportunities for critical literacy discussions.

Literacy Styles of Interpersonal Learners

It's important for highly interpersonal students to engage in literacy experiences that go beyond the traditional image of the literate person

107

sitting alone at a desk or in a chair reading a book. These students need to read in a social setting. Such a setting might include comfortable chairs, pillows, and carpeting, where several students can gather around a single book and read it together. Or students might read their own books separately, but be able to read aloud excerpts, or make comments to the others as the need to share arises without being disciplined for "disturbing others" (those who do not wish to be disturbed could read in a quieter setting). Opportunities should be provided for students to share their reading experiences with other kids in casual and comfortable settings such as book clubs and discussion groups. Similarly, at least some writing experiences need to be collective or cooperative rather than solitary efforts. Contexts that are particularly suitable might include a "storyboarding session" of students writing a screenplay, or a group project involving a collective declaration of principles for a social cause.

For Further Study

- Set up a "writing for social action" center in the classroom or school, where students can gather to focus their writing efforts on some objective that will further social justice, environmental action, consumer protection, world peace, health care, or some other worthy social goal. Provide postal and e-mail addresses, Web site listings, and other references for students to write to. Create a display area for students to show their communications and the responses they receive. Periodically hold discussion groups where students can talk about what it feels like to use the written word to cause social change. Observe how students begin to think differently about the world and about themselves as writers as they go through this process.

- Survey the various forms of written text that your students are exposed to during the school day. How do these texts mirror (or not mirror) the racial, ethnic, gender, religious, and sexual preference identifications of the students? What are the students own feelings and attitudes about the way in which their social worlds are (or are not) reflected in the material they read? How do the texts students read in school compare culturally to the texts they are exposed to outside of school?

- Create a phonics program based on words that have special social meaning to your students. Adapt Paulo Freire's general approach to using socially relevant words to generate phonetic sounds and new combinations of words to read and write (see Freire, 1998, pp. 80-110).

8

Speaking Out About the Oral Basis of Reading and Writing

In Molière's 18th-century play *The Middle Class Gentleman*, the main character, Monsieur Jourdain, asks his philosophy teacher for help in composing a love letter to "a lady of great quality." The philosopher asks Jourdain if he wants the letter to be written in verse. He replies, "No." How about prose? "No." When told by the teacher that it must be in either verse or prose, the Monsieur seems incredulous: "There is nothing but prose or verse?" he asks. When told that this is indeed the case, Jourdain then asks: "And when one speaks, what is that then?" The philosophy master answers: "Prose." Jourdain replies: "What! When I say, 'Nicole, bring me my slippers, and give me my nightcap,' that's prose?" The philosopher answers: "Yes, sir." Monsieur Jourdain finally exclaims: "By my faith! For more than forty years I have been speaking prose without knowing anything about it, and I am much obliged to you for having taught me that" (Act 2, Scene 4).

Like Molière's middle-class gentleman, we have *all* been speaking prose our entire lives (or at least the better part of it). And for those who are beginning to read and write, the ability to speak such prose puts them way ahead in the literacy game, compared with someone who has never learned to speak or use language at all. Think about it. Even people who may not be able to read or write a single word have the ability to *speak* thousands of different words and know what they mean. They can orally construct complex sentences with elaborate syntax and intricate meanings. They're able to tailor their speech to all sorts of pragmatic situations (for example, saying "excuse me!" when bumping into a person on the street, or "blast it!" when accidentally pounding their thumb with a hammer). In the course of learning to speak, they've been exposed to an enormous range of subtle sounds while hearing other people talk, and have learned to separate out and articulate just those particular sounds that are required in order to make meaningful communications to a person speaking the same language. Already, they've done at lot of homework in preparing for literacy. They have a hands-on knowledge of phonology, syntax, semantics, and pragmatics, all of which will come in very handy in the course of learning to read and write.

Of course, it's not possible to turn one's oral language on like a spigot and have it spill out onto the printed page fully formed (although there are methods and technologies that come very close to this, which we will explore later in this chapter). I've sometimes fantasized about how wonderful it would be if, in the style of the Sunday comics, we were able to speak and have our language simultaneously printed above us in giant balloons that we could read at our leisure. Alas, while virtually everyone in our culture learns to speak fluently without direct instruction, such is not the case with the development of literacy. We don't learn to read and write nearly as easily as we learned to speak. But we should take a cue from the ease with which oral language is mastered in childhood and build on what an individual already knows about language in helping that person learn how to read and write.

The Oral Roots of Literacy

The reasons for building on the oral roots of literacy are well grounded. Oral language has had an enormous head start over written language in evolution and history. We've talked far longer as a species than we've written and read. The first human language emerged roughly 150,000 years ago in East Africa, while written language is only about 6,000 years old (Dreifus, 2001). That means that 96 percent of our history with language has been solely of the oral variety. While we can never know what most of this oral language tradition consisted of, we can get a sense of its richness by surveying the oral traditions of the roughly 5,000 languages that currently exist in the world. For most of human history cultures have passed on significant knowledge—histories, genealogies, folk tales, religious ideals, ritual formulas, social compacts, knowledge of flora and fauna, and much more—by conveying it orally to the next generation. And as literacy emerged during the past few thousand years, the links with oral language have in many cases remained very strong. We must remember that many of the greatest works of civilization, from the *Old Testament* and the *Iliad* and *Odyssey*, to the Indian classic epic *Mahabharata* and the Islamic *Koran*, were first orally transmitted, and only later put into print form.

The act of reading itself has, for most of its short existence, been tied to speaking. During antiquity and medieval times, most people read books out loud, even when reading by themselves (McLuan, 1965). In fact, it was so common to read out loud in antiquity that Saint Augustine in his famous autobiographical *Confessions* (written in the fourth century C.E.), went out of his way to point out how his mentor Saint Ambrose did not move his lips when he read, suggesting that this may have been because he wanted to save his voice, or wished to avoid being pestered by questions from people overhearing his reading (Saint Augustine, 1992).

These connections between oral and written language are manifest in the brain's organizational structure. While visual (written) language has emerged out of broader oral language functions and to some extent has carved out its own specialized neurological regions as a result of both genetic and environmental factors, there is still a great deal of overlap in the brain's circuitry between auditory and visual linguistic areas (Strauss, 1998; Castro-Caldas, Petersson, Reis, Stone-Elander, & Ingvar, 1998; Chee, O'Craven, Bergida, Rosen, & Savoy, 1999). We know that children who have significant oral language difficulties often encounter later problems with reading and writing (Roth & Speece, 1996). Interestingly, research in the field of developmental dyslexia suggests individuals with severe reading difficulties show marked underactivation in those areas of the brain having to do with phonology (Shaywitz et al., 1998). While knowledge of the sounds of oral language is not in itself sufficient to provide a basis for discriminating phonological sounds in reading, it certainly is one important prerequisite. Early childhood development studies suggest that oral language and phonological sensitivity are important emergent literacy skills for the development of reading (Lonigan, Burgess, & Anthony, 2000). Children who have not been exposed to a language-rich environment where they can hear subtle differences between words will be ill prepared for the phonological tasks necessary for learning to read. Moreover, if a child is struggling to sound out a word like *bat* and has never heard the word and doesn't know what it means, it is much less likely that he will succeed in decoding the word (Whitehurst & Lonigan, 1998). Early childhood developmental studies indicate that those kids who are most successful in becoming literate are those who develop proficiency in "literate language," that is, talking in a way that mirrors the language of the schoolteachers and school texts (Michaels, 1981; Pellegrini, Galda, Bartini, & Charak, 1998).

Children's oral language capacities also function to deepen thought processes that are instrumental in developing writing competence. Vygotsky (1962) pointed out that a child's early egocentric speech is not simply an immature form of socialized speech, but rather an important precursor of inner speech—the child's ability to think in words. He wrote that "a thought may be compared to a cloud shedding a shower of words" (p. 150). In a sense, Vygotsky is talking here about the writer's (and thinker's) *voice*, akin, perhaps at a less lofty level, to the voice of the Muse in literature. Children's self-talk processes that occur in the course of play activities will, over time, become internalized and function as an inner commentator that can develop into the highly sophisticated mechanisms of a mature writer's voice. Saul Bellow, the 1976 Nobel prize winner in literature, once wrote: "I suppose that all of us have a primitive prompter or commentator within, who from earliest years has been advising us, telling us what the real world is. There is such a commentator in me. I have to prepare the ground for him. From this source come words, phrases, syllables, sometimes . . . whole paragraphs fully punctuated" (John-Steiner, 1985). British writer Margaret Drabble observed: "I hear all my sentences out loud. All of it. I can hear it being said in my voice, of course" (John-Steiner, 1985). Other writers, like American poet Amy Lowell, speak more of a voiceless commentary: "I do not hear a voice, but I do hear words pronounced, only the pronouncing is toneless. The words seem to be pronounced in my head, but with nobody speaking them" (Ghiselin, 1960). These accounts of mature writers reveal the significant oral language links that continue to exist at the highest levels of literacy.

Sounding Out About Letters and Sounds

If students can distinguish between the 44 phonemes in the English language, and can hear and show how each one sounds when combined with the others, then they have accomplished a great deal toward becoming literate even before they've encountered *any* of the visual letter forms of written language. Some research suggests that phonemic awareness is the best single predictor of how easily students will learn to read (Sensenbaugh, 1996). There are a wide range of phonemic awareness activities that will sensitize students to the sounds of language, to sound-letter correspondences, and to such skills as the ability to hear the fine distinctions between phonemes such as "p" and "b," or "sh" and "th." Here are a number of strategies:

- Have students listen to and practice poems, songs, tongue twisters, and other oral language genres that are rich with alliteration in particular sounds or sound combinations. For example, the tongue twister "Sally sells seashells down by the seashore" can help students distinguish between the "s" sound and the "sh" sound.

- Provide plenty of exposure to rhymed verse, where students can hear similar sounds and sound patterns in juxtaposition: Hickory, dickory, *dock*/the mouse ran up the *clock*.

- Play games where words are divided into their syllables. For example, the teacher says a polysyllabic word, and the student repeats the word while clapping out the syllables.

- Dedicate each day to a different phoneme and engage in activities based on that particular sound or, as is done on the PBS television show *Sesame Street*, have each day "sponsored" by a different letter of the alphabet or phoneme, and generate activities and games from that particular source.

- Create silly rhymes with your students based upon different letter-sound combinations. For example, for the sound *ack*: "I ate a Big Mac/On the railroad track/And fell on my back/And made a big quack!"

- Make up different playful chants with funny words that empha-size the sounds of the different phonemes (*a* says "aaa . . . " like *aardvark/ b* says "buh" like *Beetlejuice/* etc.).

- Read story books that have strong phonemic content, including the books of Dr. Seuss and books like *Bowl Patrol!* by Marilyn Janovitz and *Where Did Josie Go?* by Helen Buckley.

For other ideas, games, and activities, there are a range of books and resources available (see Adams, Foorman, Lundberg, and Beeler, 1997; Blevins, 1999).

Learning to Read and Write Words by Ear

Prior knowledge of words and their meanings—a good oral vocabulary—is a very useful prerequisite to launching into the experience of reading and writing. Consequently, any program that provides students with plenty of exposure to spoken words through discussions, conversations, dialogues, lectures, storytelling, and plays, as well as through having books read to them on a regular basis, will help create a strong foundation for literacy acquisition. And this process begins from the very beginning of life. Studies indicate that a child's later academic achievement can be predicted simply on the basis of the *number* of words they hear spoken during the first year of life (Blakeslee, 1997). Students should have frequent opportunities to use the words they've heard in a variety of settings including telling their own stories, giving extemporaneous talks, leading discussions, sharing during show-and-tell, making up speeches, telling jokes and riddles, and engaging in other oral language activities. There is concern among some professionals that so much attention has been given to the teaching of reading and writing, especially during the early years when children are developing their oral language capacities, that oral activities like those listed above are being seriously neglected. This neglect can even hamper children's speech development, which, in turn, can undermine later literacy development (Thornton, 2002).

As students begin to make the transition from oral language to written language teachers should make primary use of words from the student's own oral vocabulary. Ashton-Warner's organic reading method, which asks students for the words they would like to be able to read and write, is one significant program that maintains the vital connections between oral and print language (Ashton-Warner, 1986). Another helpful approach that keeps the oral-print connection alive is the use of invented spellings (also called "temporary spelling") in conjunction with a student's writing (Bissex, 1985). In invented spelling, students spell a word they are writing the way they *think* it's supposed to be spelled.

Research in this area suggests that children go through distinct stages as they create their own spellings for words they know orally (Lutz, 1986). At first, in the precommunicative stage, students use letters from the alphabet with no letter—sound correspondence (the word monster might be spelled *evijxwp*). Then, in the semi-phonetic stage, they begin to understand that letters stand for certain sounds, but only in a rudimentary way (*monster = mtr*). The third stage, the phonetic stage, reveals the full flowering of a child's use of his or her "linguistic ear" in rendering written words as they really sound—this is the stage where oral language and written language meet most fully in a child's spelling (*monster = monstur*). After this, in the transitional stage, a child's spelling begins to incorporate visual patterns from words they already know how to spell (*monster = monstore*). Finally, in the fifth stage, the child arrives at the conventional stage and uses the standard English orthographic system and its basic rules to spell the word conventionally (Armstrong, 1990). Research suggests that children who were encouraged to use invented spelling in their writing wrote significantly longer and more elaborate stories and scored higher on spelling and reading tests than children who were not so encouraged (Clark, 1988). As students write with their invented (or temporary) spellings, encourage them to share their own ideas about why they spelled a word a certain way.

Reading and Writing Sentences Out Loud

In working with sentences for use in grammar lessons, vocabulary building, or other purposes, employ sentences taken from the oral speech of the students rather than a textbook. It is far more inviting for a student to pick out the verb in a sentence that he has just spoken ("Are we going to study grammar today, Mrs. Sumner?") than to do so in an artificial sentence written by an educator he has never met ("The children played on the sidewalk"). A teacher might simply tape record the conversation of students coming into the classroom, and then replay the conversation, picking out specific sentences to write on the blackboard or overhead as material for looking at active-passive construction, parts of speech, and other grammar objectives. Or students might themselves be encouraged to take tape recorders with them and record speech samples, which can then be brought back to supply the lesson with applicable material. This approach allows students to see that grammar is not some stuffy discipline unconnected with their lives, but is integral to their daily conversations with others. Such a method also allows the opportunity to examine dialect, slang, and other regionalisms and idiosyncracies of speech, along with their appropriateness or inappropriateness to given social settings.

Reading and Writing Text with the Ear in Mind

When I taught in special education programs for elementary school and middle school students, I often included personal one-to-one time with my students where they would meet with me in a corner of the classroom and dictate stories, monologues, jokes, or anything else that they wanted to say to me (including a narrative of what had happened to them during the day). I sat at a typewriter and typed furiously as they spoke. Fortunately, I had set up my own dissertation-typing business while in college (I typed around 125 words per minute), so it wasn't a strain for me to keep up with them. The part I enjoyed the most was watching them look at the words as they were being typed on the page, and seeing them light up with excitement as they began to realize that these were their own spoken words appearing "magically" out of the typewriter. Some students would have fun with this, and try to outrace me, or would start and stop their words in short spurts, making sure that I wrote exactly what they had said, or would try to trick me by speaking unintelligible speech sounds. Other students would simply take the finished pages in their hands and stare at them in disbelief and wonder: "These are *my* words? These are *my* words!" We would then use this text in reading lessons, vocabulary development, spelling, and for other literary purposes (including incorporation into our class newspaper).

Nowadays, this ability to transform a student's own spoken words directly into text is made easier by the existence of word processing programs, as well as by software such as IBM's Via Voice, which eliminates the go-between and directly transfers the student's voice into printed words on the screen. Such technologies bring alive my old fantasy that all students should have the joy of seeing the words coming out of their mouths and turning into print. Literacy programs need to include plenty of opportunities for students to see their own spoken words transformed into written text in some of these ways.

Once students begin reading and writing, they should also be encouraged to "listen" to the different "voices" expressed in books, and also to the inner voices inside of them that are the accumulation of all the voices they have ever heard in their lives. These voices can be drawn upon when they are writing stories, narratives, or other literary pieces. Here are a number of ways to do this:

- Have students keep a notebook where they record interesting snatches of speech they overhear during the course of a day (from family, friends, media, etc.). These can then be incorporated into their own writing as dialogue or narrative.

- Ask students to talk in someone else's "voice" and then have them write this dialogue down on paper just as it sounds: "Talk like your mother when she asks you to take out the garbage." "Talk like the president of the United States."

- Provide students with a prewriting time when they simply close their eyes and listen to their inner voice (or voices), and then invite them to write down on paper what they hear in their mind's ear.

- Model the experience of writing by doing some of your own writing, as a teacher, on the blackboard. As you do this, talk out loud about what's going through your mind as you write: "Okay class, now I want to write a sentence that will make people pay attention to the importance of taking good care of their health. So what am I going to say? Hmmmm . . . I'm thinking about writing a sentence with an exclamation point, like 'People!' [write it down, then erase it]. No, maybe that's coming on too strong. Maybe something like 'How long do you want to live?' [write it down]. Yes, that'll grab people's attention. And then maybe, 'Do you think you have a say in how long you'll live?' No, I want to make this more of a statement: 'You have a BIG say in how long you will live.'" Then, encourage students to talk out loud as they write (perhaps initially in pairs so they can monitor each other), and even tape record them so they can get direct feedback on the inner processes they use while writing.

- Encourage students to get involved in the oral interpretation of literature. Select pieces and passages from literature that are particularly well suited to dramatic interpretation, such as famous speeches, monologues from plays, and dialogue from novels and short stories. Then ask students to perform these pieces before the class. The National Forensic League (125 Watson Street, P.O. Box 38, Ripon, Wisconsin, 54971; 920-748-6206) provides opportunities for competition between high schools on a regional and national level in dramatic and humorous interpretation of texts as well as extemporaneous speaking, debate, and original oratory.

- Have students watch closed-captioned programs that include both the oral language and the printed language at the bottom of the screen.

Using Books and Other Literacy Materials with Strong Oral-Language Foundations

When thinking about stocking a library or literacy program with books and other materials that are linked to oral language, it may be helpful to conceptualize a spectrum of resources that extends from printed texts devoid of any real writer's voice on the one hand, to purely oral language materials on the other hand. Starting from this print-rich/voice-poor side of the continuum, it bears stating that *most* of the written materials that students are exposed to in school are of this type, and thus are *least* suited to the needs of a curriculum that acknowledges the important role that oral language has in literacy development. I am speaking here of textbooks and worksheets, which make up from 75 to 90 percent of classroom instruction in the United States (Tyson & Woodward, 1989).

One of the biggest problems with textbooks and worksheets, in general, is that they are often written by committees and don't have a personal voice that speaks directly to the reader. An important implication of a strong oral language component in literacy development is that students be provided with texts that include these intimate voices. One study of high school history students suggested that readers are more highly motivated to explore the content of history textbooks when "someone with, like, a life wrote it" (Paxton, 1997). Better than textbooks, of course, are real books, especially fictional works written with a distinct authorial voice, or books, which include a number of voices represented by different characters from different walks of life.

If we continue along the spectrum from print to oral materials, we arrive at books that have a distinct auditory component. These include books that come with computer chips that tell the story audibly; interactive software programs, where readers can click onto dialogue, sentences, and individual words and hear them said aloud; and books that have accompanying cassette or CD narration. Teachers can easily make these talking books by reading short books into a tape recorder, and then attaching the tape to the book for use by students who want to read the book and hear it read at the same time. Students might also be interested in reading and taping books for younger students, or for each other.

Toward the other end of the spectrum we have print-poor/voice-rich materials represented by books on tape, which can be listened to without any reference to print. Organizations like Recordings for the Blind and Dyslexic (20 Roszel Road, Princeton, New Jersey, 08540; 800-221-4792) provide a wide variety of such literacy materials on tape for those who qualify under diagnostic guidelines for dyslexia. Especially compelling in this category are authors reading their own work. Finally, at the very end of the continuum are recordings of purely oral performances such as famous speeches and orations, collected folk tales from oral traditions, stand-up comedy routines, storytelling, narratives, and related oral language materials.

Literacy Styles for the Learner with Strong Oral Language Skills

Our culture and school system tend to value the literate person who reads quickly by gathering meaning from a page in a rapid visual scan. The ubiquity of speed-reading schools and speed-reading programs over the past several decades testifies to this cultural bias. In school, one of the most popular periods of the day among literacy-minded educators is "Sustained *Silent* Reading." Our culture tends to devalue the individual who speaks out loud or whispers as she reads. We call this tendency "subverbalization" and have even considered it a sign of reading pathology. And yet, as we noted earlier with Augustine, reading in ancient times was almost always associated with reading out loud. Hence, we ought to provide individuals—especially those with strong oral language abilities—with the opportunity to speak the words that they read. (I'm not speaking here about formal "reading groups" where each student takes turns reading aloud. These conditions often create paralyzing pressure for shy students, creating additional roadblocks to reading.) Perhaps the educator might provide an area of a classroom or school for "out loud readers." Such readers should not only be able to read, whisper, or mumble the words they read but should also be allowed to "think out loud" about the material as they read as well as participate in discussion groups both before and after reading.

Similarly, in writing activities, it's very important for some students to talk out loud as they write, perhaps forming the sounds of words they are attempting to spell, or speaking aloud a stream of words as they search for the right one ("he was happy . . . no . . . content . . . no . . . satisfied . . . yes!"), or talking themselves through a plot sequence or a sequence of ideas ("I want the hero to get in trouble first . . . and then . . . have somebody come to save him . . . "). Instead of viewing the highly oral writer/reader as a chatterbox or a subverbalizer, we should admire the fact that she continues to maintain a strong connection to the deep and fertile soil of humanity's oral language tradition.

For Further Study

- Have students create text directly from their spoken language, either using speech recognition software, or by having their words transcribed from a tape recorder or from direct dictation. This text can then be edited (and perhaps illustrated) by the students, and turned into book form either through the students' own book-making activities, or by having the material professionally bound at a media center.

- Set up a "literacy out loud" center, which might include an area where students are allowed to read out loud, think out loud, and write out loud, as well as a listening station with excellent literature on tape and recordings of important speeches, orations, folk tales, and more. Such a center might also sponsor book readings, oral interpretation of great literature, poetry readings, storytelling events, and other experiences that bring together oral language with text.

- Do a research project where you ask your students what they are thinking about as they read and write, and what form it takes (words, visual images, etc.). Record their responses and transcribe them. Then assemble a variety of descriptions that great writers have given of how they think as they read and write (such as the passages by Saul Bellow, Margaret Drabble, and Amy Lowell highlighted earlier), and put the two sets of descriptions (great writers and your students) together in a bulletin board display, a research paper, or some other type of project ("How Our Class and Great Writers Think When They Read and Write").

9

Opening the Book of Nature

Normally, we think of literacy as something entirely separate from nature. Words clearly don't tweet like birds, moo like cows, or blow in the wind like flowers, nor do they water our gardens or form mountainous vistas across the wide horizon. Words are the tools of culture—abstract representations that we use to understand and control the world around us. And yet, in another sense, words and literacy have a central relationship to the natural world, insofar as they have emerged *from* nature and still have deep roots in its primeval soil. One neuroscientist has suggested, for example, that humans were pre-adapted neurologically for reading through, among other things, the ancient skill of animal tracking, which could be considered the "reading" of hoof or paw prints (Varney, 2002). Linguists are able to track the migrations of preliterate Indo-European tribes by examining Indo-European root words that relate to nature (Indo-European is the foundational language for many modern languages, including English). There is no word for *sea* in this proto-language, for example, suggesting that these were landlocked people. We know that they came from cooler climes, because they have a root word *sneigh*, which evolved into our own word *snow*. As humans acquired literacy, the connections between words and nature continued to be very strong. In ancient Egypt, the need to control the flooding of the Nile using vast irrigation systems led to more complex social organization and the need to develop a system of *writing* to handle the increased workload. The Greeks had a myth for the origin of their alphabet based in part on natural forces. According to this myth, Cadmus brought the alphabet and literacy to Greece after he slew a dragon (an embodiment of brute nature), and then took the dragon's teeth and planted them in the soil, whereupon sprang up an army of men, whose survivors helped him found the city of Thebes. Literacy, thus is represented in terms of the human struggle to control, and thereby surmount, nature.

Nature and Literacy: The Living Links

We can see the early links between nature and words mirrored in the lives of children just beginning to acquire literacy skills. A young child is alive with the rhythms and sensations of nature—she revels in watching a bird fly, smelling a flower, feeling the wind against her face, observing a squirrel eating a nut. These experiences captivate the child in a way that words, lying lifeless on the page, simply cannot.

However, as the child is introduced to printed words and discovers the mysteries they can reveal about the world around her, they too become imbued with a kind of magical natural quality. American writer Eudora Welty wrote about having to grow out of the belief that words were themselves living organisms: "It had been startling and disappointing to me to find out (at a young age) that story books were not natural wonders, coming up of themselves like grass" (Hidalgo, 2001). British critic John Ruskin told of how in his childhood the word *crocodile* with its long series of letters had something of the long sinuous, jointed appearance of the reptile itself (Werner, 1973). French philosopher Jean-Paul Sartre wrote about his first realization that his mother was reading a book to him: "I didn't recognize her speech. Where had she got that assurance? A moment later, I realized: it was the book that was speaking. Frightening sentences emerged from it: *they were real centipedes* [italics are mine], they swarmed with syllables and letters, stretched their diphthongs, made the double consonants vibrate" (Sartre, 1964, p. 29). In his autobiography, English biographer and critic Edmund Gosse wrote about his belief as a child that magic could make the material in books come alive: "I persuaded myself that if I could only discover the proper words to say or the proper passes to make, I could induce the gorgeous birds and butterflies in my Father's illustrated manuals to come to life and fly out of the book, leaving holes behind them" (Piaget, 1975, p. 135).

These allusions to nature and literacy continue into our adulthood. In our daily speech we make frequent use of metaphors that bring these two elements together. We speak of "reading the book of nature." We talk about finding word "roots." We refer to letters as having "stems." Allan Metcalf, executive secretary of the American Dialect Society, compared the development of language itself to nature: "It may help to think of language as a great field of word plants. Whenever most people focus their attention on one subject, it's like a great dose of fertilizer and rain on that portion of the field. Existing words grow and flower into new meanings. Nouns sprout verbs" (Ringle, 2001).

There are even suggestions that the brain itself codes linguistic information according to naturalistic categories. Pinker (1994, p. 314) writes about aphasics who can use nouns for living things but have trouble with nouns for nonliving things, or those who have trouble with nouns for anything but animals, or patients who cannot name objects typically found indoors (see, for example, Moss & Tyler, 1997). Because nature is fundamental to our survival, I think it's worth speculating upon the possibility that linguistic categories for natural things may be somehow more firmly entrenched in our brains than the more recent cultural overlaying of nonliving objects and things. And if this is true, then approaches to literacy acquisition that emphasize nature and natural phenomena are likely to bear much fruit in producing successful readers and writers. The rest of this chapter will explore several ways to make this happen.

Learning Letters and Sounds Through Nature

The 44 phonemes of the English language are sounds made by human beings which, when combined with each other, create more complex sounds that represent the many things and processes that make up our world. As human sounds, they represent sounds of nature, because human beings are animals (albeit of a highly intelligent variety) living on this planet alongside other animals who make their own unique sounds. Consequently, at their base (putting aside for the moment their representational significance), the 44 phonemes can be regarded as nature sounds sharing the same auditory qualities as the purring of cats, the barking of dogs, the growling of bears, and even the babbling of brooks and the patter of rain. This observation gives us an important clue as to how phonetic sounds might be introduced in a naturalistic way. Consider, for a moment, the "oo" sound in *tool*. Are there any other creatures besides humans who make this sound in nature? How about owls? (Hooo! Hooo!). Think about the initial consonant *b* as in *basket*. What things in nature might make this sound? How about the "buh . . . buh . . . bubbling" of swamp gas? Or possibly certain species of frogs ("buuuh . . . buuuh . . . ")? Blending sounds together brings in more possibilities. What happens, for example, when we combine the "b" in *baby* with the "a" sound in *last*? We get: "baaaa . . . baaaaa . . . " Are there sheep around here somewhere?

I think by now you have a sense of how to proceed in building a phonics program based on nature sounds. When some students hear phonetic sounds pronounced for the first time in traditional reading and literacy programs, they hear sounds that are disconnected from their actual experience, that have a weird, artificial quality about them. If, however, they are pronounced initially as nature sounds, then the student recognizes them immediately as sounds he or she already knows about and loves. Because so many children are already tuned in to the wide diversity of sounds in nature, they will often be able to hear nature sounds in the 44 phonemes better than the teacher. We need to give them a chance to generate their own nature associations. Often writers have their own unusual associations between nature and specific phonemes. Novelist Vladimir Nabokov wrote in his autobiography that he associated the long "a" sound with the tint of weathered wood, the "z" sound with a thundercloud, and the letter *k* with the buckle-berry plant (Carter, 1998). If students are having difficulty with teacher-imposed nature phonemes, it's especially important for them to create their own internal associations.

Similarly, in learning the visual forms of the letters, using natural forms that look like letters of the alphabet may succeed in winning over the nature-loving student. There is, for example, a wonderful book, *The Butterfly Alphabet* by Smithsonian naturalist Kjell B. Sandved, that consists of a series of photographs of butterfly wings that have inscribed on them natural markings that look very much like each letter of the alphabet as well as the numbers from zero to nine (he searched for these forms in nature over a period of 24 years). As students begin to learn the letters, they can be taken on walks in nature and asked to look for shapes and forms of the different letters A to Z (and perhaps even take pictures of them to bring back to the classroom and share as "Our Neighborhood Nature Alphabet").

The Natural Way to Master Words

For students who love nature and are just learning to read and write, it seems obvious that a large part of their vocabulary should be related to nature. Such a list might be compiled, for example, during a walk with the students outside of the school building. As they walk, the students might be asked to name the many natural things they see, and as they call them out, the teacher can write each one down on a card and give it to the student involved. Once back in the classroom, each student might assemble his or her cards into a story or poem. It's important that the students don't simply go out in nature and automatically label everything they see—a process that might serve to compress nature into the tight little boxes of words without nature itself being addressed and appreciated. Gary Snyder quotes the 12th century Zen Buddhist philosopher Dogen, who said: "To see a wren in a bush, call it 'wren' and go on walking is to have . . . seen nothing. To see a bird and stop, watch, feel, forget yourself for a moment, be in the bushy shadows, maybe then feel 'wren'—that is to have joined in a larger moment with the world" (Snyder, 2000).

Just as phonemes are related to sounds in nature, individual words can also be linked directly to the sounds that occur in nature. In a nature-focused literacy program, many of a student's first words might consist of onomatopoetic words based in nature, such as *buzz*, *splash* and *murmur*. Writer and educator Joseph Bruchac explains to his students how the word for *crow* in the Native American language of Abenaki is also the sound it makes ("gah-gah") and the seagull's name is *kah-ahk*. He suggests that students write down "the sound of a bird song, the sound of a pine tree's breath as the wind shushes through it on a high ridge. They can collect a whole new vocabulary of words given them by the wind. Then ask them to write a poem making use of one or more of those new words" (Bruchac, 2000, p. 33). Here are a number of other ways to bring words and nature together:

- Ask students to think of nature words that are used to express human experiences, as for example, when we speak of a person "crowing" about an achievement, or someone who is being "dogged" by their past.

- Have students collect specialized words related to their favorite animal or plant. Use guides such as *Roadside Plants and Flowers* by Marian S. Edsall, or the *National Audubon Society Field Guild to North American Birds*, for help in identifying and naming specific plants and/or animals.

- Take students on a gardener's adventure to explore "word roots" (bring your own gardener's gloves and trowel). Use a carrot or other root plant (with its leaves still intact) for your demonstration and place a number of word labels on the leaves (e.g., *ambulance, ambulatory, amble*), while attaching their word root (*ambu*) to the root itself. To make it even more realistic, replant it with the labels intact, and take the class out to dig it up!

Working with Wild Sentences

As students explore the grammatical structure of sentences, they should be using sentences that come directly from observations in nature. Again, a walk in nature is recommended so the students can formulate their own sentences from what they hear, see, feel, touch, and smell: "I see a robin flying swiftly through the sky." "The wind is screaming in my ear." "Smells of daffodils and roses taste delicious to my nose buds." These sentences can then be brought back into the classroom and looked at in terms of sentence structure, or other syntactic or semantic objectives. For example, the teacher might ask students to substitute other adverbs to describe how the bird is flying, or to think of other verbs to suggest what the wind is doing, or to examine the use of metaphor in linking smells to tastes. Noam Chomsky's syntactic diagrams (see Figure 5.1) look very much like the branches of a tree or plant, and might be presented in this way using a naturalistic diagram format where the branching of verb phrases, noun phrases, and so forth, might be shown artistically as the shooting up of branches or, inversely, as the putting down of roots. Here are a few other ideas:

- When working with a specific skill like punctuation, have students write sentences that are questions they have about nature ("Why is the sky blue?"), or strong statements about nature (or ecology) that demand exclamation marks ("I hate it when people throw garbage out of their cars!").

- When teaching about prepositional phrases, have students act out the various phrases in nature while the teacher holds up a large card with the appropriate phrase ("Now I want you to go around the lilac bush. Now walk onto the lawn. Now jump over the log").

- Ask students to observe events happening in nature, and to describe "subject-object" happenings ("I see a squirrel eating a nut—the subject is squirrel, the nut is the object").

Reading and Writing Gardens of Text

Pulitzer-prize winning poet Gary Synder contrasts good writing and extraordinary writing by using the metaphor of a garden: "Ordinary Good Writing is like a garden that is producing exactly what you want, by virtue of lots of weeding and cultivating. What you get is what you plant, like a row of beans. But really good writing is both inside and outside the garden fence. It can be a few beans, but also some wild poppies, vetches, mariposa lilies, ceanothus, and some juncos and yellow jackets thrown in. It is more diverse, more interesting, more unpredictable" (Snyder, 2000, p. 3). When reading or writing text with students who have naturalistic proclivities, use these kinds of outdoor metaphors, and encourage students to use them in critiquing or analyzing what makes for good text, great text, or even poor text:

"This short story I'm writing has too many weeds in it! I've got to pull a few out and plant some better root words!" "This textbook chapter reads like a barren wasteland with just a few burned-out trees on it!"

Make the focus of writing assignments, whenever possible, relate directly to nature. Even if the students live in an urban environment, they can still write about the birds flying around the buildings, the trees in planters on the sidewalk, the pets being walked by their owners, the animals they visit at the zoo, and the flowers they see in parks. Whether in an urban or rural environment, one good way to begin would be to have students take a walk outside with a small notebook and pencil in hand, and as they see things in nature that attract them, have them write down words, phrases, sentences, and even visual sketches that describe what they observe and how they feel or think about what they are experiencing. Then, back in the classroom, they can share their words with the class, and perhaps get encouragement to expand their observations and reflections into a larger project, such as a poem, story, science project, nature essay, or ecology experiment. Here are a number of other ways to help focus students' writing about nature:

- Using the movie *Honey, I Shrunk the Kids* or the book *Powers of Ten* as a starting point, invite students to imagine that they have shrunk to the size of an ant or microbe and then write about a plot of land from this very small point of view.

- Invite students to write "green essays" that propose solutions to specific community environmental problems such as polluted local beaches, unclean air from local factories, or dying trees in a neighborhood park. The students can then submit their essays to newspapers or journals.

- Have students go to a specific place in nature for 5 to 10 minutes a day for a week or longer and write down their observations in a notebook.

- Let students select a favorite animal, plant, or other object in nature and write through its voice ("I am the wind . . . blowing through all the cracks and crevices of life, nothing can stop me, I am irresistible"). As a subcategory of this strategy, have the students pick an endangered species and write as if voicing their despair, fears, needs, and hopes.

- Have students write nature haiku. One resource for information and examples of nature haiku is William J. Higginson's *Haiku World: An International Poetry Almanac.*

- When reading a text that takes place in nature, have students close their eyes and experience the scene as fully as possible, imagining what the scene looks like, smells like, sounds like, and feels like. Let students investigate specific flora or fauna mentioned in a text, especially those plants or animals that are unfamiliar to them.

- Find an animal for each student to care for in school (or suggest they use their pet at home), and have students keep an ongoing journal about their experience of feeding and caring for it.

- Read to students from great nature writers such as Henry David Thoreau, John Muir, and Annie Dillard, and then have them respond with nature writing of their own.

- Provide students with reproductions of well-known photos or paintings depicting nature scenes (try Ansel Adams's photos of Yosemite Park, or British artist J. M. W. Turner's famous paintings of seascapes and sunsets) and ask them to create captions, poetry, stories, or essays based on these images.

For further strategies, ideas, and resources on reading and writing about nature with students, see Christian McEwen and Mark Statman's excellent anthology of writings, *The Alphabet of the Trees* (McEwen & Statman, Eds., 2000).

Books and Other Literacy Materials for the Naturalist

There is a wide variety of resources to choose from in selecting books and literacy materials to use with students who love nature. There are books that are specific to animals (books on bats, turtles, lizards, bees), books on taking care of pets, books for garden care, books on ecology and saving the environment, books on how animals build their homes, books on stargazing, and books on keeping track of the weather, to name just a very few nonfiction nature categories. In fiction there is a similarly enormous list to choose from in children's literature, from

Mother Goose and Beatrix Potter, to *Where the Wild Things Are*, *Charlotte's Web*, and the children's board book *Moo, Baa, LA LA LA!* Workman Publishing Company puts out a series of books that include naturalist tools attached to each book, including *The Bug Book/Book and Bottle*, *The Bird Book and the Bird Feeder*, and the *Backyard Explorer Kit* (which comes equipped with a heavy plastic envelope for gathering leaves and needles, and an album to mount them in). Then there is the genre of nature periodicals and magazines such as *National Geographic*, *National Geographic for Kids*, and *Ranger Rick*, a wealth of nature guides, maps, and field guides to specific regions, parks, or landmarks, as well as lots of photography books that focus on specific plants, animals, ecologies, or regions. Add to this all the great classics of nature literature for adults, including the poetry of John Keats ("Ode to a Nightingale") and Wallace Stevens ("Thirteen Ways of Looking at a Blackbird"), the novels of Herman Melville (*Moby Dick*) and Jack London (*The Call of the Wild*), and the nature essays of Henry David Thoreau (*Walden*) and Annie Dillard (*Pilgrim at Tinker's Creek*), to name just a few, and you have quite a collection of literacy materials to attract the attention of those who are naturalistically inclined.

Literacy Styles of the Nature Lover

Sitting in a chair at a table or desk in a classroom with fluorescent lighting and no windows is certainly one of the worst places for highly naturalistic students to do their reading and writing, and yet all too many nature lovers spend their time engaged in literacy activities in these enclosed artificial surroundings. To get students closer to nature, consider creating a reading and writing area outside the school building, using weatherproof tables or park benches (and paperweights to keep materials from blowing away in the wind). At the very least, let students read and write in an area with large windows, natural lighting, plants, and perhaps even animals in the room. One reading program even has children reading to pets as a way of improving their (the children's) reading skills. It's called R.E.A.D., Reading Educational Assistance Dog (www.therapyanimals.org/read/index.htm).

You might consider creating a "Naturalist's Reading and Writing Room" with an aquarium, terrarium, hanging plants, potted plants on the floor and tables, and other environmental touches to enhance the reading and writing environment. As we've noted above, whenever possible, have students engage in their writing activities while out in nature. The ideal image of a naturalist student engaged in literacy activities is of a person walking through the woods or meadows or hills with a backpack containing writing implements and a journal for the student's own field notes, observations, poetry, or nature reflections, and appropriate reading material (nature guide, nature poetry).

For Further Study

- Create a "Nature Phonics" program by taking the 44 phonemes of English (or those that are especially problematic to the students) and linking each to a nature sound. If possible, enlist the help of your students in creating this system. Include visual images of each thing in nature making its sound, and use bodily-kinesthetic gestures to accompany the nature sounds. Then, when students are having trouble with specific phonetic sounds while reading, they can be prompted using these "nature phonemes."

- Lead your students on a literary nature hike, where together you take time out to read classic nature literature, write about what you see in nature, discuss environmental issues, and engage in other eco-literary activities. If you have the opportunity, go to a natural spot in your area that has been enshrined in poetry, story, or essay, and read and discuss the work at its point of origin.

- Put together a collection of appropriate literacy materials having to do with nature, and make them available to the students in your program. If possible, engage the students themselves in the process of choosing these materials.

- Create a "Words and Nature" display area or activity center in your classroom that includes interesting nature words (for example, animal names such as "Hammerkop," "colobus," and "antechinus"), famous quotations from nature poets or naturalists, as well as concrete nature poetry (e.g., Reinhard Döhl's poem "Pattern of Poem with an Elusive Intruder," which is arranged in the shape of an apple; its entire text consists of the word *apfel* [apple in German] repeated over and over again, except for one intruding word: *würm*). Include activity cards with instructions for students to create their own crazy animal names, concrete poetry, or quotations about nature.

Conclusion

While scientific studies proliferate to pin down the specific mechanisms of reading and writing, I am committed to the belief that literacy is nothing short of a miracle—our contemporary version of magic. To be able to see worlds and create universes through the mere act of looking at and making marks on a page, if you really start to think about it long and hard, seems incredible—a conjurer's art or a medium's genius. In this context, it seems remarkable to me not that so many people struggle to learn how to read and write, but that so many are actually able to do so. This is especially true given the bare bones way in which so many students are normally taught literacy skills, where worksheets and workbooks abound, and little attention is focused on all of the marvelous capacities that have pre-adapted the brain for literacy: using gestures, emotions, and musical intonation to communicate, creating picture languages, developing vast oral traditions, and deploying innate logical structures in using words, among many other capacities.

I think that as teachers of literacy skills, we need to approach our craft not as a mandate that must be imposed upon all—at the risk of students being labeled "reading disordered" or "learning disabled"—but rather as a sacred charge that we are given by society to respectfully hand to a new generation, with the wisdom of all that has gone before us to guide us in our work. As such, we need to be gentle in our approach, knowing how delicate and specialized the mechanisms for literacy actually are for each student, and we need to be broad-minded, and even humble, in our attitude, knowing that reading and writing are but a small subset of the vast range of modes of human symbol-making. We have made the mistake of isolating literacy from this rich heritage, putting it in a bare room with only a blackboard (or computer screen), an alphabet poster, and some workbooks to keep it company, an environment where it can hardly hope to have the chance to thrive. Instead, we need to reconnect literacy to all that has come before it, and all that is still connected to it in the brain, by creating environments where reading and writing skills are nourished and supported with music, art, nature experiences, logical analyses, dramatic performances, oral recitations, emotional expression, social interaction, and a wide range of other creative nutrients. I hope that this book has been a help to you in making some of these connections, and I wish you the very best success in empowering your students with the miraculous gifts of the Literacy Lion, which is a very mysterious and wonderful beast indeed!

References

Adams, M. J., Foorman, B. R., Lundberg, I., & Beeler, T. (1997). *Phonemic awareness in young children: A classroom curriculum.* Baltimore, MD: Paul H. Brookes, Inc.

Allott, R. (2000, April). *Gestural equivalence of language.* Conference paper, Gesture Meaning and Use, Oporto, Portugal. http://www.percepp.demon.co.uk.

Angell, R. (2001, August 6). Postscript: Eudora Welty. *The New Yorker,* 30.

Armstrong, T. (1990, February). Speak and spell. *Parenting Magazine, 4(1),* 36–38.

Armstrong, T. (1997). *The myth of the A.D.D. child: 50 ways to improve your child's behavior and attention span without drugs, labels, or coercion.* New York: Plume.

Armstrong, T. (1999a). *7 kinds of smart: Discovering and identifying your many intelligences.* New York: Plume.

Armstrong, T. (1999b). *ADD/ADHD alternatives in the classroom.* Alexandria, VA: ASCD.

Armstrong, T. (2000a). *Multiple intelligences in the classroom* (2nd ed.). Alexandria, VA: ASCD.

Armstrong, T. (2000b). *In their own way: Discovering and encouraging your child's multiple intelligences.* New York: Tarcher/Putnam.

Arnheim, R. (1969). *Visual thinking.* Berkeley, CA: University of California Press.

Ashton-Warner, S. (1986). *Teacher.* New York: Simon & Schuster.

Atterman, J. (1997). *Reading strategies for beginning and proficient readers.* Bloomington, IN, ERIC Clearinghouse on Reading English and Communication. (ERIC Document Reproduction Service No. ED416447.)

Ayer, A. J. (1952). *Language, truth, and logic.* New York: Dover Publications.

Baker, S. K., Simmons, D. C., & Kameenui, E. J. (1998). Vocabulary acquisition: Research bases. In D. C. Simmons & E. J. Kameenui (Eds.), *What reading research tells us about children with diverse learning needs* (pp. 183–217). Mahwah, NJ: Lawrence Erlbaum Associates.

Barclay, K. D., & Walwer, L. (1992, May). Linking lyrics and literacy through song picture books. *Young Children, 47(4),* 76–85.

Barsch, R. H. (1974). *Ray H. Barsch presents "... and sometimes y." 109 fun ways to enjoy and improve spelling in the classroom.* Canoga Park, CA: The Ray Barsch Center for Learning.

Beeman, M. J., & Bowden, E. M. (2000). The right hemisphere maintains solution-related activation for yet-to-be-solved problems. *Memory and Cognition. 28(7):* 1231–1241.

Bentley, G. E., Jr. (2001). *The Stranger from Paradise: A Biography of William Blake.* New Haven, CT: Yale University Press.

Bettelheim, B. (1981). *On learning to read: The child's fascination with meaning.* New York: Alfred A. Knopf.

Bickerton, D. (1982, July). Creole languages. *Scientific American, 249,* 116–122.

Bindman, D. (Ed.). (2000). *William Blake: The complete illuminated books.* London: Thames & Hudson.

Bissex, G. L. (1985). *Gnys at wrk: A child learns to write and read.* Cambridge, MA: Harvard University Press.

Blakeslee, S. (1997, August 1). Studies show talking with infants shapes basis of ability to think. *The New York Times,* p. A14.

Blevins, W. (1999). *Phonemic awareness activities for early reading success (grades K–2).* New York: Scholastic.

Borduin, B. J., Borduin, C. M., & Manley, C. M. (1984, March). The use of imagery training to improve reading comprehension of second graders. *Journal of Genetic Psychology, 155(1),* 115–118.

Brodkey, H. (1985, November 24). Reading, the most dangerous game. *The New York Times Book Review,* pp. 1; 44–45.

Bruchac, J. (2000). The land keeps talking to us. In C. McEwen & M. Statman (Eds.), *The alphabet of the trees.* New York: Teachers & Writers Collaborative.

Bryant, P. E., MacLean, M., Bradley, L. L., & Crossland, J. (1990). Rhyme and alliteration, phoneme detection, and learning to read. *Developmental Psychology, 26(3),* 429–438.

Campbell, L., Campbell, B., & Dickinson, D. (1995). *Teaching and learning through multiple intelligences.* Boston: Allyn & Bacon.

Carbo, M., Dunn, R., & Dunn, K. (1986). *Teaching students to read through their individual learning styles.* Boston, MA: Allyn & Bacon.

Carmon, A., Nachshon, I., and Starinsky, R. (1976). Developmental aspects of visual hemifield differences in perception of verbal material. *Brain and Language, 3,* 463–469.

Carroll, J. A. (1991, October). Drawing into meaning: A powerful writing tool. *English Journal. 80(6),* 34–38.

Carter, R. (1998). *Mapping the mind.* Berkeley, CA: University of California Press.

Castro-Caldas, A., Petersson, K. M., Reis, A., Stone-Elander, S., & Ingvar, M. (1998). The illiterate brain. Learning to read and write during childhood influences the functional organization of the adult brain. *Brain, 121(Pt. 6),* 1053–1063.

Chee, M. W., O'Craven, K. M., Bergida, R., Rosen, B. R., & Savoy, R. L. (1999). Auditory and visual word processing studied with fMRI. *Human Brain Mapping, 7(1),* 15–28.

Chiarello, C., Liu, S., & Faust, M. (2001). Bihemispheric sensitivity to sentence anomaly. *Neuropsychologia, 39(13),* 1451–1463.

Chomsky, N. (1957). *Syntactic structures.* The Hague, The Netherlands: Mouton & Co.

Chomsky, N. (1994–1995, December-January). An interview with Noam Chomsky. *The Reading Teacher, 48(4),* 328–333.

Clark, L. K. (1988). Invented versus traditional spelling in first graders' writings: Effects on learning to spell and read. *Research on the Teaching of English, 22 (3),* 218–308.

Cohen, H., Douaire, J., & Elsabbagh, M. (2001). The role of prosody in discourse processing. *Brain and Cognition, 45(1–2):* 73–82.

Coles, G. (1998). *Reading lessons: The debate over literacy.* New York: Hill & Wang.

Coles, G. (2000). *Misreading reading: The bad science that hurts children.* Portsmouth, NH: Heinemann.

Comber, B., Thomson, P., & Wells, M. (2001, March). Critical literacy finds a "place": Writing and social action in a low-income Australian grade 2/3 classroom. *The Elementary School Journal, 101(4),* 451.

Coney, J (1998). Hemispheric priming in a reading task, *Brain and Language. 62(1),* 34–50.

Coney, J. (2002). Probing hemispheric processes in an on-line reading task. *Brain and Language, 80(2),* 130–141.

Coney, J. & Evans, K. D. (2000). Hemispheric asymmetries in the resolution of lexical ambiguity. *Neuropsychologia, 38(3),* 272–282.

Cordoni, B. (1981, January). Teaching the LD child to read through visual imagery. *Academic Therapy, 16(3),* 327–331.

Creighton, D. C. (1997, October). Critical literacy in the elementary classroom. *Language Arts, 74(6),* 438–445.

Cripe, F. F. (1986). Rock music as therapy for children with attention deficit disorder: An exploratory study. *Journal of Music Therapy, 23(1),* 30–37.

Darwin, C. (1910). *Expression of the emotions in man and animals.* New York: D. Appleton & Co.

Day, T. A. (2000). *Lesbian and gay voices: An annotated bibliography and guide to literature for children and young adults.* Westport, CT: Greenwood Publishing Group.

Dennison, P. & Dennison, G. (1994). *Brain gym: Teachers edition.* Ventura, CA: Edu-Kinesthetics.

Deshler, D. D., Ellis, E. S., & Lenz, B. K. (1996). *Teaching adolescents with learning disabilities: Strategies and methods.* Denver, CO: Love Publishing Company.

Donahue, P. L., Finnegan, R. J., Lutkus, A. D., Allen, N. L., & Campell, J. R. (2001). *The nation's report card: Fourth-grade reading 2000.* Washington, DC: U.S. Department of Education.

Douglass, F. (1997). *Narrative of the life of Frederick Douglass.* New York: Signet.

Dreifus, C. (2001, October 30). A conversation with John McWhorter: How language came to be, and change. *The New York Times.*

Embick, D., Marantz, A., Miyashita, Y., O'Neil, W., & Sakai, K. L. (2000, May 23). A syntactic specialization for Broca's area. *Proceedings of the National Academy of Sciences,* 97(11): 6150–6154.

Esrock, E. J. (1986). The inner space of reading: Interviews with John Hawkes, Carlos Fuentes, and William Gass on visual imaging. *Journal of Mental Imagery, 10(2),* 61–68.

Ferguson, J. (2002, September). *Dyslexia and brain scans: A criticism of design.* Paper presented to the Luria Conference, Moscow, Russia. (For reprint contact: scancode@wireweb.net)

Fernald, G. (1988). *Remedial techniques in basic school subjects.* Austin, TX: Pro-Ed.

Fisher, D., & McDonald, N. (2001, Fall). The intersection between music and early literacy instruction: Listening to literacy! *Reading Improvement, 38(3),* 106–115.

Fisher, D., McDonald, N., & Strickland, J. (2001, Spring). Early literacy development: A sound practice. *General Music Today, 14(3).*

Flesch, R. (1986). *Why Johnny can't read: And what you can do about it.* New York: HarperCollins.

Freire, P. (1998). Education for critical consciousness. In A.M. Freire, & D. Macedo (Eds.), *The Paulo Freire Reader* (pp. 80–110). New York: Continuum.

Freire, P. (2000). *Pedagogy of the Oppressed.* New York: Continuum.

Freud, S. (1966). Psychopathology of everyday life. In A. A. Brill (Ed.), *The Basic Writings of Sigmund Freud* (pp. 35–180). New York: Modern Library.

Fulbright, R. K., Jenner, A. R., Mencl, W. E., Pugh, K. R., Shaywitz, B. A., Shaywitz, S. E., et al. (1999, November-December). The cerebellum's role in reading: A functional MR imaging study. *American Journal of Neuroradiology, 20 (10),* 1925–1230.

Gailey, S. K. (1993, January). The mathematics-children's literature connection. *Arithmetic Teacher, 40(5),* 258–261.

Gambrell, L. B., & Bales, R. J. (1986, Fall). Mental imagery and the comprehension-monitoring performance of fourth- and fifth-grade poor readers. *Reading Research Quarterly, XXI(4),* 454–464.

Gardner, H. (1974). *The shattered mind.* New York: Vintage.

Gardner, H. (1983). *Frames of mind: The theory of multiple intelligences.* New York: Basic Books.

Gardner, H. (1993). *Multiple intelligences: The theory in practice.* New York: Basic Books.

Gardner, H. (1999). *Intelligence reframed: Multiple intelligences for the 21st century.* New York: Basic Books.

Gattegno, C. (1985). *The common sense of teaching reading and writing.* New York: Educational Solutions.

Geschwind, N. (1979, September). Specializations of the human brain. *Scientific American, 241(3),* 180–199.

Geschwind, N. (1982). Why Orton was right. *Annals of Dyslexia, 32,* 13–30.

Ghiselin, B. (1960). *The creative process.* New York: Mentor.

Gilles, C. (1998, September). Constant connections through literature—using art, music, and drama. *Language Arts, 76(1),* 67–75.

Glazner, G. M. (Ed.). (2000). *Poetry slam: The competitive art of performance poetry.* San Francisco, CA: Manic D Press.

Goldman, S. R., & Rakestraw, J. A., Jr. (2000). Structural aspects of constructing meaning from text. In M. L. Kamil, P. B. Mosenthal, P. D. Pearson, & R. Barr (Eds.), *Handbook of reading research, Vol. III.* Mahwah, NJ: Lawrence Erlbaum Associates.

Goodman, Y., & Marek, A. (1996). *Retrospective miscue analysis: Revaluing readers and reading.* Katonah, NY: Richard C. Owen.

Greenwald, J. (1999, July 5). Retraining your brain: How one company is using a new neurological theory to ease language and reading problems. *Time Magazine, 154(1),* 52+.

Grodzinsky, Y. (2000). The neurology of syntax: Language use without Broca's area. *Behavioral and Brain Sciences, 23,* 1–71.

Hannaford, C. (1995). *Smart moves: Why learning is not all in your head.* Arlington, VA: Great Ocean Publishers.

Harp, B. (1988, February). Why are you doing guided imagery during reading time? *The Reading Teacher, 41(6):* 588–590.

Hidalgo, B. (2001, Summer). Eudora Welty, master storyteller. *Authors Guild Bulletin,* 9.

Hoerr, T. (2000). *Becoming a multiple intelligences school.* Alexandria, VA: ASCD.

Horwitz, B., Rumsey, J. M., & Donohue, B. C. (1998, January 18). Functional connectivity of the angular gyrus in normal reading and dyslexia. *Proceedings of the National Academy of Sciences, USA, 95,* 8939–8944.

Houston, J. (1982). *The possible human.* New York: Tarcher/Putnam.

Howard, M. (1982). Utilizing oral-motor feedback in auditory conceptualization. *Journal of Educational Neuropsychology, Vol. 1,* 32–38.

Indefrey, P., Brown, C. M., Hellwig, F., Amunts, K., Hertzog, H., Seitz, R. J., et al. (2001, May 8). A neural correlate of syntactic encoding during speech production. *Proceedings of the National Academy of Sciences, USA, 98(10),* 5933–5936.

Irlen, H. (1991). *Reading by the colors: Overcoming dyslexia and other reading disabilities through the Irlen method.* New York: Berkley.

Jackson, D. D. (1995, January). Believe it or not, Rip was almost as odd as his "items." *Smithsonian Magazine,* 91–98.

Jackson, P., & Forrester, P. (1994). *The pop-up book: Step-by-step instructions for creating over 100 original paper products.* New York: Henry Holt.

James, W. (1910). *Principles of psychology,* (Vol. 2). New York: Henry Holt.

Janson, H.W. (1969). *History of art,* 5th Ed. New York: Harry Abrams.

John-Steiner, V. (1985). *Notebooks of the mind: Explorations of thinking.* New York: Harper & Row.

Johnston, K. (2001, June). Broken fingers: Classic Maya scribe capture and polity consolidation. *Antiquity, 75(288),* 371–381.

Joseph, R. (1992). *The right brain and the unconscious.* New York: Plenum Press.

Joyce, J. (1969). *Finnegans wake.* New York: Viking.

Kimelman, M. D. (1999). Prosody, linguistic demands, and auditory comprehension in aphasia. *Brain and Language, 69(2),* 212–221.

Kircher, T. T., Brammer, M., Tous Andreu, N., Williams, S. C., & McGuire, P. K. (2001). Engagement of right temporal cortex during processing of linguistic context. *Neuropsychologia, 39(8),* 798–809.

Koch, K. (1970). *Wishes, lies, and dreams: Teaching children to write poetry.* New York: Vintage.

Kolb, G. R. (1996, September). Read with a beat: Developing literacy through music and song. *The Reading Teacher, 50(1),* 76–77.

Landis, T., Graves, R., & Goodglass, H. (1982). Aphasic reading and writing: Possible evidence for right hemisphere participation. *Cortex, 18(1),* 105–112.

Lazear, D. (1999). *Eight ways of knowing: Teaching for multiple intelligences.* Palatine, IL: Skylight.

Lerdahl, F. (2001). The sounds of poetry viewed as music. *Annals of the New York Academy of Science, 930,* 337–354.

Logan, R. K. (1986). *The alphabet effect.* New York: William Morrow.

Lonigan, C. J., Burgess, S. R., & Anthony, J. L. (2000). Development of emergent literacy and early reading skills in preschool children: Evidence from a latent-variable longitudinal study. *Developmental Psychology, 36(5),* 596–613.

Lopate, P. (1977). The moment to write. In B. Zavatsky & R. Padgett (Eds.), *The Whole Word Catalogue 2.* New York: McGraw-Hill.

Ludwig, C., & Herschell, P. (1998, February). The power of pedagogy: Routines, school literacy practices, and outcomes. *Australian Journal of Language and Literacy, 21(1),* 67–83.

Lutz, E. (1986). Invented spellings and spelling development. (ERIC Document Reproduction Service No. ED272922.)

Macrine, S. L. (1997, Spring). Toward a dialogical mediated action approach to reading. *Education, 117(3),* 386–396.

Marchand-Martella, N., Miller, T. L., & MacQueen, C. (1998, January). Graphic organizers. *Teaching Pre-K–8, 28(4),* 46–48.

McAdam, E. L., & Milne, G. (1995). *Johnson's dictionary: A modern selection.* London: Cassell.

McCall, A. L., & Ford, M. P. (1998, Spring). Why not do something? Literature as a catalyst for social action. *Childhood Education, 74(3),* 130–135.

McClatchy, J. D. (1995, March 27). Braving the elements. *The New Yorker,* 49–61.

McCracken, R. A., & McCracken, M. J. (1998). *Stories, songs, and poetry to teach reading and writing.* Winnipeg, Manitoba: Peguis.

McEwen, C., & Statman, M. (Eds.). (2000). *The alphabet of the trees.* New York: Teachers & Writers Collaborative.

McGill, D. C. (1987, October 23). Painting saves a child. *The New York Times.*

McGuinness, D. (1985). *When children don't learn: Understanding the biology and psychology of learning disabilities.* New York: Basic Books.

McLuan, M. (1965). *The Gutenberg galaxy.* Toronto, Ontario: University of Toronto Press.

Meikle, J. (2001, January 12). Dyslexia therapy "getting results." *Manchester Guardian.*

Meltzoff, A. N. (1999). Origins of theory of mind, cognition and communication. *Journal of Communication Disorders, 32(4),* 251–269.

Michaels, S. (1981). "Sharing time": Children's narrative styles and differential access to literacy. *Language in Society, 10,* 423–442.

Michel, F., Hanaff, M. A., & Intrillgator, J. (1996). Two different readers in the same brain after a posterior callosal lesion. *Neuroreport, 7(3),* 786–788.

Montessori, M. (1973). *The secret of childhood.* New York: Ballantine.

Moss, H. E., & Tyler, L. K. (1997). A category-specific impairment for non-living things in a case of progressive aphasia. *Brain & Language, 60(1),* 55–58.

Motluk, A. (2001, January 27). Read my mind. *New Scientist,* 22–25.

Nash, G. (1974). *Creative approaches to child development with music, language, and movement: Incorporating the philosophies of Orff, Kodaly, and Laban.* Van Nuys, CA: Alfred Publishing Company.

Nelson, K. (1998). *Developing students' multiple intelligences.* New York: Scholastic.

Neruda, P. (1977). *Memoirs.* New York: Farrar, Straus, Giroux.

Nicolson, R. I., & Fawcett, A. J. (1999, September). Developmental dyslexia: The role of the cerebellum. *Dyslexia: An International Journal of Research and Practice, 5(3),* 155–177.

Noden, H., & Moss, B. (1995, March). Nurturing artistic images in student reading and writing. *The Reading Teacher, 48(6),* 532–534.

Odean, K. (1997). *Great books for girls: More than 600 books to inspire today's girls and tomorrow's women.* New York: Ballantine.

Odean, K. (1998). *Great books for boys: More than 600 books for boys 2 to 14.* New York: Ballantine.

Olshansky, B. (1994, September). Making writing a work of art: Image-making within the writing process. *Language Arts, 71(5),* 350–356.

Paul, D. G. (2000, November). Rap and orality: Critical media literacy, pedagogy, and cultural synchronization. *Journal of Adolescent and Adult Literacy, 44(3),* 246.

Paxton, R. J. (1997). "Someone with like a life wrote it": The effects of a visible author on high school history students. *Journal of Educational Psychology, 89(2),* 235–250.

Pellegrini, A. D., Galda, L., Bartini, M., & Charak, D. (1998). Oral language and literacy learning in context: The role of social relationships. *Merrill-Palmer Quarterly, 44(1),* 38–54.

Piaget, J. (1975). *The child's conception of the world.* Totowa, New Jersey: Littlefield, Adams & Co.

Pinker, S. (1994). *The language instinct.* New York: William Morrow.

Prichard, A., & Taylor, J. (1980). *Accelerated learning: The use of suggestion in the classroom.* Novato, CA: Academic Therapy Publications.

Proust, M. (1934). *Remembrance of things past: Vol. 1.* (C. K. S. Moncrieff, Trans.). New York: Random House.

Raschke, D., Alper, S., & Eggers, E. (Winter, 1999). Recalling alphabet letter names: A mnemonic system to facilitate learning. *Preventing School Failure, 43(2),* 80.

Rico, G. L. (1983). *Writing the natural way: Using right-brain techniques to release your expressive powers.* Los Angeles: J. P. Tarcher.

Ringle, K. (2001, November 10). Them's fightin' words: War lingo rushes to the front. *Washington Post,* p. C01.

Rivard, J. D., & Bieske, G. B. (1993, March). Using contemporary music themes to increase adolescents' confidence and reading fluency. *Journal of Reading, 36(6),* 492–493.

Robinson, A. (1995). *The story of writing.* London: Thames and Hudson.

Rose, D. S., Parks, M., Androes, K., & McMahon, S. D. (2000, September). Imagery-based learning: Improving elementary students' reading comprehension with drama techniques. *Journal of Educational Research, 94(1),* 55.

Roth, F. P., & Speece, D. L. (1996, Fall). Unresolved mysteries: How do metalinguistic and narrative skills connect with early reading? *Journal of Special Education, 30(3),* 257–277.

Rozin, P., Poritsky, S., & Sotsky, R. (1971, March 26). American children with reading problems can easily learn to read English represented by Chinese characters. *Science, 171,* 1264–1267.

Saint Augustine. (1992). *Confessions.* Oxford, England: Oxford University Press.

Sakai, K. L., Hashimoto, R., & Homae, F. (2001). Sentence processing in the cerebral cortex. *Neuroscience Research, 39(1),* 1–10.

Sansavini, A., Bertoncini, J., & Giovanelli, G. (1997). Newborns discriminate the rhythm of multisyllabic stressed words. *Developmental Psychology 33,* 3–11.

Sartre, J. P. (1964). *The words.* New York: Fawcett.

Sensenbaugh, R. (1996, June). *Phonemic awareness: An important early step in learning to read.* ERIC Clearinghouse on Reading, English, and Communication Digest #119. (ERIC Document Reproduction Service No. EDO-CS-96-13.)

Shamrock, M. (1986, February). Orff Shulwerk: An integrated foundation. *Music Education Journal, 72,* 51–55.

Shaywitz, S. E., Escobar, M. D., Shaywitz, B. A., Fletcher, J. M., & Makuch, R. (1992, January 16). Evidence that dyslexia may represent the lower tail of a normal distribution of reading ability. *The New England Journal of Medicine, 326(3),* 145–150.

Shaywitz, S. E., Shaywitz, B. A., Pugh, K. R., Fulbright, R. K., Costable, R. T., Mencl, W. E., et al. (1998, March 3). Functional disruption in the organization of the brain for reading in dyslexia. *Proceedings of the National Academy of Sciences, USA, 95(5),* 2636–2641.

Shibahara, N., & Lucero-Wagoner, B. (2001). Access to perceptual and conceptual information in the left and right hemisphere. *Perceptual and Motor Skills, 93(3),* 649–659.

Simpson, J. R., Snyder, A. Z., Gusnard, D. A., & Raichle, M. E. (2001). Emotion-induced changes in human medial prefrontal cortex: I. During cognitive task performance. *Proceedings of the National Academy of Sciences, USA,* 98(2), 683–687.

Smith, F. (1996). *Reading without nonsense* (3rd ed.). New York: Teachers College Press.

Snyder, G. (2000). Language goes two ways. In C. McEwen & M. Statman (Eds.), *The alphabet of the trees* (pp. 1–5). New York: Teachers & Writers Collaborative.

Sperber, D., & Wilson, D. (2002). Pragmatics, modularity, and mind reading. *Mind and Language, 17(1),* 3–33.

Steiner, R. (1976). *Practical advice to teachers.* London: Rudolf Steiner Press.

Steiner, R. (1983). *An introduction to eurythmy.* Herndon, VA: Anthroposophic Press.

Steiner, S. F. (2001). *Promoting a global community through multicultural children's literature.* Greenwood Village, CO: Libraries Unlimited.

Strauss, E. (1998, May 8). Writing, speech separated in split brain. (Research on how the human brain organizes components of language.) *Science, 280(5365),* 827–828.

Studdert-Kennedy, M. (Ed.). (1983). *Psychobiology of language.* Cambridge, MA: MIT Press.

Talcott, J. B., Wilton, C., McLean, M. F., Hanson, P. C., Rees, A., Green, G. R., et al. (2000, March 14). Dynamic sensory sensitivity and children's word decoding skills. *Proceedings of the National Academy of Sciences, USA, 97(6):* 2952–2957.

Thiessen, D., Mathias, M., & Smith, J. (1998). *The wonderful world of mathematics: A critically annotated list of children's books in mathematics* (2nd ed.). Reston, VA: National Council of Teachers of Mathematics.

Thornton, K. (2002, January 11). Early years reading and writing hampers speech. *Times Educational Supplement.*

Tims, S., & Williams, C. (1992). Emergent writing skills of kindergarten students: The effectiveness of guided imagery. *Dissertation Abstracts International, 53, 08A.* (1992): 2678.

Tu, Wei. (1999, December). Using literature to help children cope with problems. ERIC Digest D148, ED436008.

Tyson, H., & Woodward, A. (1989, November). Why students aren't learning very much from textbooks. *Educational Leadership, 47,* 14–17.

Vaneechouette, M., & Skoyles, J. R. (1998). The memetic origin of language: Modern humans as musical primates. *Journal of Memetics—Evolutionary Models of Information Transmission, 2(2),* 84–117.

Van Strien, J. W., Stolk, B. D., & Zuiker, S. (1995). Hemisphere-specific treatment of dyslexia subtypes: Better reading with anxiety-laden words? *Journal of Learning Disabilities, 28(1),* 30–34.

Varney, N, R. (2002). How reading works: Considerations from prehistory to the present. *Applied Neuropsychology, 9(1),* 3-12.

Venis, S. (2001, March 17). Complex writing systems problematic for people with dyslexia. *Lancet, 357(9259),* 861.

Viau, E. A. (1998, March). Shades of meaning: Using color to enhance reading. *Journal of Adolescent and Adult Literacy, 41(6),* 476–477.

Vogeley, K. et al. (2001). Mind reading: Neural mechanisms of theory of mind and self-perspective. *Neuroimage, 14(1),* 170–181.

von Hilshimer, G. (1970). *How to live with your special child*. Washington, DC: Acropolis.

Vygotsky, L. S. (1962). *Thought and language*. Cambridge, MA: MIT Press.

Wade, N. (2001, October 4). Researchers say gene is linked to language. *New York Times*, p. A1.

Wallace, R. R. (1992). *Rappin' and rhymin': Raps, songs, cheers, smart-rope jingles for active learning*. Tucson, AZ: Zephyr Press.

Werner, H. (1973). *The comparative psychology of mental development*. New York: International Universities Press.

West, T. G. (1997). *In the mind's eye: Visual thinkers, gifted people with dyslexia and other learning difficulties, computer images and the ironies of creativity*. Amherst, NY: Prometheus Books.

Whitehurst, G. J. & Lonigan, C. J. (1998, June). Child development and emergent literacy. *Child Development, 69(3)*, 848–872.

Wilson, F. R. (1998). *The hand: How its use shapes the brain, language, and human culture*. New York: Pantheon.

Wise, B. (2002, January). Kid-calculated reading levels. *Teaching Pre-K–8, 32(4)*, 62–63.

Woodcock, R. Clarke, C. R., & Davies. C. O. (1968). *Peabody rebus reading program*. Circle Pines, MN: American Guidance Service.

Wright, W.L. (1991). Using imagery as a prewriting strategy to enhance creativity. *Masters Abstracts International, 35 (03)*, 0630.

Yopp, R. H., & Yopp, H. K. (1997). *Oopples and boo-noo-noos: Songs and activities for phonemic awareness*. New York: Harcourt Brace.

Zentall, S., & Kruczek, T. (1988). The attraction of color for active attention-problem children. *Exceptional Children, 54(4)*, 357–362.

Index

In this index, page locators followed by *f* indicate a figure found in the text.

About the Author

Thomas Armstrong, Ph.D., is the author of 11 books, including the ASCD books *Multiple Intelligences in the Classroom*, 2nd ed., *Awakening Genius in the Classroom*, and *ADD/ADHD Alternatives in the Classroom*, and the books *7 Kinds of Smart* and *In Their Own Way* (both published by Putnam-Penguin). He lives in Sonoma County, California, and can be reached through his Web site (www.thomasarmstrong.com) at: thomas@thomasarmstrong.com or by phone: 707-894-4646 or fax: 707-894-4474. He can also be reached by mail: P.O. Box 548, Cloverdale, CA 95425.

Related ASCD Resources: Multiple Intelligences

At the time of publication, the following ASCD resources were available; for the most up-to-date information about ASCD resources, go to www.ascd.org. ASCD stock numbers are noted in parentheses.

Audiotapes

Connecting the Curriculum Using an Integrated, Interdisciplinary, Thematic Approach by T. Roger Taylor (#297093)

Teaching for Understanding Through Multiple Intelligences by Geni Boyer (#297189)

CD-ROMs

Exploring Our Multiple Intelligences (#596276)

Networks

Visit the ASCD Web site (www.ascd.org) and search for "networks" for information about professional educators who have formed groups around topics like "Multiple Intelligences," "Interdisciplinary Curriculum and Instruction," and "Language, Literacy and Literature: Whole Language Perspective and Practice." Look in the "Network Directory" for current facilitators' addresses and phone numbers.

Online Courses

Multiple Intelligences Professional Development course

Print Products

Becoming a Multiple Intelligences School, by Thomas R. Hoerr (#100006)

Multiple Intelligences and Student Achievement: Success Stories from Six Schools, by Linda Campbell and Bruce Campbell (#199274)

Multiple Intelligences in the Classroom, 2nd Edition, by Thomas Armstrong (#100041)

Videotapes

Becoming a Multiple Intelligences School Books-in-Action Video (#400213)

The Multiple Intelligences Series (#495003)

For more information, visit us on the Web (http://www.ascd.org), send an e-mail message to member@ascd.org, call the ASCD Service Center (1-800-933-ASCD or 703-578-9600, then press 2), send a fax to 703-575-5400, or write to Information Services, ASCD, 1703 N. Beauregard St., Alexandria, VA 22311-1714 USA.